COUNTERING the MASS SHOOTER THREAT

Printed in the United States.

Library of Congress Control Number: 2008933390

ISBN 978-1-5323-3173-2

Countering the Mass Shooter Threat, First Edition.

Fifth Printing, 2021.

Written and Designed by Michael Martin.

Sandy Hook. Virginia Tech. San Bernardino. Orlando. Charleston. Fort Hood. Red Lake. We've reached an era where we no longer refer to mass shootings by date or context. We simply refer to them by the name of the city or the university or the military base or the high school or the elementary school where the attack took place; no different than we refer to historic battles in far-off lands. But those battles carry exotic names like Iwo Jima, Bastogne and Hue, while the names we use to refer to mass shootings sound as though they are right down the street, and too often, they are.

Like many parents with young children, the news of Sandy Hook was a particularly difficult story to hear, and I hoped that my young sons might be oblivious to the events, even as graphic images were splashed across the nightly news. But my luck ran out several weeks after the massacre when my youngest son, who was seven years old at the time, came home from school and told me that some of his friends were talking about a "bad man that killed some kids at a school." In a soft voice, Sam asked me if I thought something like that could happen at *his* school, which happens to be a private Catholic school in my home city. I pulled him in tight, looked him in the eye and assured him that nothing like that would ever happen here, and that even if a bad guy did get into his school, our police department was so good and so fast, that it would stop the bad guy before he hurt anyone.

Of course, I was lying to him. As a dad, I was supposed to have the answers, but for that particular question, I had none. So I looked him straight in the eye ... and I lied.

In the days that followed, I spoke with my son's school and the leaders of our church to ask them, "What *is* the plan in the event of a mass shooter?" The answers that I received were, at best, incomplete or inconclusive. For example, when I asked about adding security doors or establishing some type of armed presence to protect the school, our then current principal dismissed the idea by saying, "The school needs to balance security with access." After hearing that, I remember wondering what people would think if the Department of Homeland Security had used that same argument when it came to airport or cockpit security in the aftermath of 9/11. The answer I heard from our church leaders was no better. While I was uncomfortable that I had no good answer for my son, I was even less comfortable that our school and our church had no good answer for *me*. Those unanswered questions put me on a three-year path to gather as much data about these mass shootings as possible, and to ultimately answer the question for myself and my family: *What can counter this threat?*

When I began my research, I wanted to establish a baseline. In other words, I wanted to understand exactly what constituted an "active shooting" or a "mass shooter." And I wanted to fully understand the data that had been gathered on these events from multiple sources, including the FBI and the

Department of Homeland Security. In Part One, I'll provide you with a high level summary of many of those data points, including key definitions, data trends of these events, a breakdown on where these events are occurring and even a detailed look at police response time to these shootings.

As part of my research, I also wanted to understand what factors affected the outcome at mass shootings. For example, after every mass shooting (in particular, after the Newtown shooting at Sandy Hook elementary), there was a deafening cry by gun-control advocates to ban certain classes of firearms and to reduce the number of rounds that could be stored in magazines. Gun-control advocates were driven by the belief that those changes would reduce the number of dead at mass shootings or even eliminate them all together. In addition to understanding whether those arguments were right or wrong, I also wanted to better understand whether these shooters really did gravitate toward gun-free zones as the NRA and other pro-gun organizations have claimed. Lastly, I wanted to understand how the response of potential victims affected the outcome. In other words, I wanted to understand whether pleading with the shooter, running away, hiding or fighting back changed the probability of living or dying. We'll also explore that data in Part One.

Next, I wanted to fully research the solutions being proposed by gun-control advocates to determine whether the data indicated that those solutions would work or not. For example, I wanted to better understand how many mass shootings, if any, would have been stopped if universal background checks had been the law. To answer that question, I had to dig into the source of every single firearm, for every single mass shooting since Columbine. I'll share those results with you in Part One, where I'll also answer a number of other questions that you may have about other proposed solutions.

Lastly, with all of the data that I gathered, I want to propose whatever solutions are necessary to significantly move the dial on the current trajectory of mass shootings in the U.S., ultimately saving lives. But I want to back up those solutions with hard and irrefutable data. If the data determines that one or more of the solutions proposed by gun-control advocates will work, then I am prepared to embrace those solutions. But if not, I am ready to propose something new. I'll add that what I was looking for in the data was *clear and convincing evidence*. I wasn't looking for just a single event or even a few events to prove a point or draw a conclusion. That approach is happening far too often on *both* sides of the political aisle. If I make a recommendation to institute a program or suggest to ban a particular product or eliminate a particular right, it is based upon clear and convincing evidence that those changes would have a *significant* impact. If the solution won't move the dial at all or barely make the dial quiver, then it is not a solution I am interested in.

The solutions that I'll be discussing in Part Two are comprehensive. These solutions are meant to deter potential shooters *before* they strike. They are meant to end attacks early, minimizing the number of victims *when* they strike, and save the lives of victims *after* the attack is over.

Wherever you fall on the political spectrum, I hope there is something in this book that you can use. Some of the data may call into question your own long-held beliefs. Whether you accept all of my conclusions or not, you should find something of value in my recommendations. It could be learning how to properly develop an Emergency Operations Plan (EOP) for your house of worship, school or business. Or it could be learning how to make a field expedient tourniquet or chest seal in order to protect the life of a critically injured victim if you ever find yourself at the scene of a mass shooting.

I'll close this introduction by mentioning that as a writer, one of my favorite parts of any project is the point where I begin to find images to support my writing and to help tell the story. That stage in this project, was heart-wrenching. The images of the bloody aftermath of these mass shootings, the agony in the faces of family members, the endless prayer services and the look of pure evil in the faces of these mass shooters added up to making this the most difficult project I've ever tackled. But as the father of two wonderful sons, I needed to know the answer to the question I posed earlier which is: *What can counter this threat?*

Photo by Matthew Cavanaugh

CONTENTS

→ PART ONE

WHAT HAVE WE LEARNED ABOUT MASS SHOOTERS?

Rural/Metro Ambulance

- Mass Shootings by the Numbers
- Would Reducing Magazine Capacity or Banning AR-15s Work?
- Do Gun-Free Zones Help or Hurt?
- Does Victim Response Make a Difference?
- What Are Universal Background Checks? Would They End Mass Shootings?
- No-Fly Lists and Terror Watch Lists

> *The federal government defines an active shooter as, "An individual actively engaged in killing or attempting to kill people in a confined and populated area."*
>
> *"The primary motive in these incidents appears to be mass murder; that is, the shooting is not a by-product of an attempt to commit another crime."*

DEFINITIONS

To begin, let's agree on a few definitions. The terms, *active shooter* and *mass shooting* are sometimes used interchangeably by the media, but there is actually a federal government definition for both of those terms. To start with, let's look at the federal government's definition of an active shooter. That definition states that an active shooter is "an individual actively engaged in killing or attempting to kill people in a confined and populated area." That doesn't necessarily mean that anyone was killed at an active shooting event. In fact, of the 165 shootings that the FBI categorizes as "active shootings" since 2000, no one was killed at 35 of the events, and one person was killed at each of another 32 events. So think of an active shooting event as an incident where an individual is *attempting* to kill a large number of people in a confined area, even if they weren't successful.

I think it's also helpful to understand what makes active shooting events different than other types of shootings. For that, I like to use a definition created by Dr. Pete Blair, Hunter Martaindale and Terry Nichols, who authored a document for the FBI titled, *Active Shooter Events from 2000 to 2013*. These three gentlemen explained that, "The primary motive in these incidents appears to be mass murder; that is, the shooting is not a by-product of an attempt to commit another crime." That definition is one reason why the FBI doesn't count events committed as part of gang violence, or events that occurred during a robbery or a drug crime. Those crimes get another categorization, rather than one of an active shooting event.

As mentioned, an event may fit the FBI's definition of an ASE even if no one was killed, while the FBI defines a *mass shooting* as an event where four or more people have been fatally shot, not including the shooter. In a moment, we'll review just how many of these events have occurred since Columbine.

FREQUENCY

While they remain rare, as shown on the chart below, ASEs have been on the rise since 2000. I'll add that while the trend of ASEs has been on the rise, the trend of violent crime as a whole — in particular, murders committed with firearms — has been on the decline for the past 30 years. To say that again, while active shooting events have been on the rise since 2000, violent crime as a whole has dropped year after year. So something is changing. Some new factor is at play when compared to the traditional factors that motivate the average criminal to commit a violent crime.

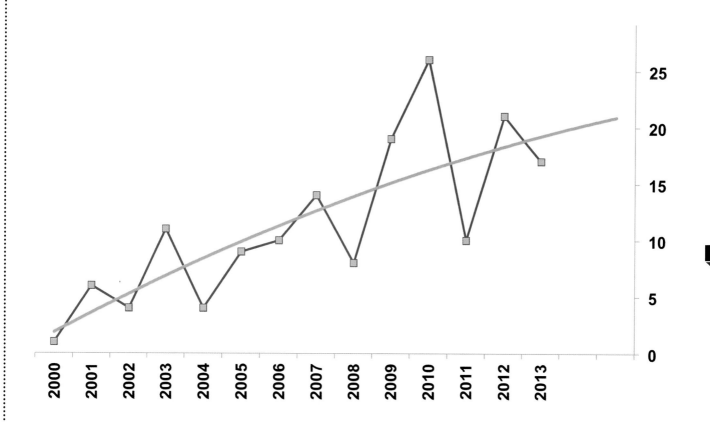

Source: Dr. Pete Blair, Hunter Martaindale and Terry Nichols, *Active Shooter Events from 2000 to 2013*.

> *"Historically, one of the central motivations in [these] cases, although not the only one, is a desire for notoriety and a desire for infamy, and now we have a setting, a cultural and social setting, where your act of multiple homicides will be known about internationally within moments. So there's a twisted incentive that didn't exist a generation ago."*
> *Dr. Reid Meloy*

Correlation With Growth of Social Media

So what's changing? Theories vary as to why the trend of ASEs is accelerating, but one of the simplest explanations is that the rise in ASEs has matched the increase in the popularity of social media such as Facebook and Twitter. So what could social media possibly have to do with an increase in active shootings? If you consider that the goal of the mass shooter is notoriety, then social media works in their favor. Social media and news alerts on smart phones guarantee that the crimes committed by mass shooters will instantly be known to millions of people around the world, and that the crime will outlive the event and the shooter. If you have doubts about that theory, think about how you found out about the shooting in Newtown or at Umpqua Community College or the shooting in San Bernardino or the shooting at the Pulse nightclub in Orlando, Florida. Like tens of millions of other people, I heard about those incidents within minutes ... by an alert on my smart phone.

Dr. Reid Meloy, a clinical professor of psychiatry at the University of California and a writer for *Psychology Today*, agrees that social media may play a part. "Historically, one of the central motivations in [these] cases, although not the only one, is a desire for notoriety and a desire for infamy, and now we have a setting, a cultural and social setting, where your act of multiple homicides will be known about internationally within moments. So there's a twisted incentive that didn't exist a generation ago."

But a link to social media may be just one part in a larger puzzle. To explain another piece of the puzzle, it's helpful to understand what's referred to as the "threshold of violence theory" which was developed more than two decades before the Columbine shooting.

The Threshold of Violence Theory

In his 1978 research paper, *Threshold Models of Collective Behavior*, Dr. Mark Granovetter set out to explain why a person would do something that seemed so completely out of the ordinary with who they were or what society deemed as acceptable. Granovetter's model used riots as an example since riots involved not only violent instigators but often encompassed seemingly ordinary people. The same model could also be applied to more benign social processes such as a decision to spread a rumor, leave a party or join a strike. Granovetter theorized that the likelihood that someone will join in on one of those social processes is based upon the individual's personal "threshold," which he described as the number (or the proportion) of other people who will need to have already engaged in the activity before the new individual will also join in. In other words, Granovetter's model explained that these social processes were often influenced as much by the collective behavior of a larger group as they were influenced by the preference of the individual.

In his riot model (and in an excellent interpretation of the model by Malcolm Gladwell for *The New Yorker*), Granovetter suggested that riots are

■ *The rise in active shooting events has matched the rise in popularity of social media such as Facebook and Twitter. If you consider that the goal of the active shooter is notoriety, then social media works in their favor. Social media and news alerts on smart phones guarantee that the crimes committed by mass shooters will instantly be known to millions of people, and that the crime will outlive the event and the shooter.*

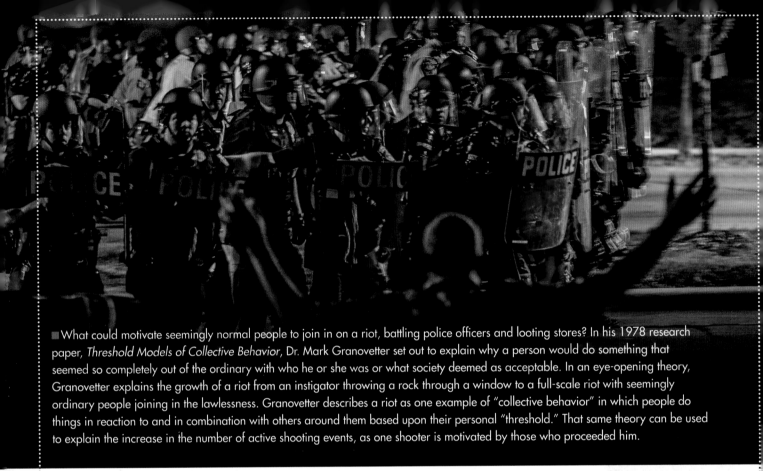

■ What could motivate seemingly normal people to join in on a riot, battling police officers and looting stores? In his 1978 research paper, *Threshold Models of Collective Behavior*, Dr. Mark Granovetter set out to explain why a person would do something that seemed so completely out of the ordinary with who he or she was or what society deemed as acceptable. In an eye-opening theory, Granovetter explains the growth of a riot from an instigator throwing a rock through a window to a full-scale riot with seemingly ordinary people joining in the lawlessness. Granovetter describes a riot as one example of "collective behavior" in which people do things in reaction to and in combination with others around them based upon their personal "threshold." That same theory can be used to explain the increase in the number of active shooting events, as one shooter is motivated by those who proceeded him.

initiated by people with a threshold of zero, or instigators who are willing to throw a rock through a window at the slightest insult or provocation. Next comes the person with a threshold of one, who will throw a rock if someone else went first. After that, a person with a threshold of two may join in, but only after seeing two others already engaged in the riot. Their reaction may be, "I didn't start it but I'll join in." The riot grows and spreads from person to person until eventually it engulfs individuals who would never have considered *starting* a riot, but who are now willing to join with the mob, throwing garbage cans through store fronts and looting property ... but only if everyone around them was already destroying and stealing property. In the view of a person who would normally have a threshold of 100, the riot has just become socially acceptable. While the threshold model effectively explains how a riot can progress from an instigator throwing a rock through a window to a full-scale riot with seemingly ordinary people joining in the lawlessness, Malcolm Gladwell also uses the model to theorize why active shooting events are on the rise by viewing these shootings as another type of social process susceptible to collective behavior. Gladwell views the Columbine shooters as the start of the "riot," each with a threshold of zero. Since then, we've been seeing a "slow-motion, ever-evolving riot, in which

Columbine Copycats

74

53
PLOTS OR
THREATS
THWARTED
BY LAW
ENFORCEMENT

21
ATTACKS

**89
DEAD**

126
WOUNDED

14
Attacks were
planned to fall on the
anniversary of the
Columbine shooting.
12 attacks were
thwarted, while 2
were successfully
carried out on
different dates.

13
Plotters indicated
that their goal was
to outdo the body
count of Columbine
shooters Eric Harris
and Dylan Klebold.

"The problem is not that there is an endless supply of deeply disturbed young men who are willing to contemplate horrific acts. It's worse. It's that young men no longer need to be deeply disturbed to contemplate horrific acts."
Malcolm Gladwell, The New Yorker

each new participant's action makes sense in reaction to and in combination with those who came before." In other words, the Columbine attackers threw the first rock, which led to rocks being thrown by others with a threshold of one or two or three. The effect of the pair's example was to make it possible for people with far higher thresholds — as Gladwell describes them, "boys who would ordinarily never think of firing a weapon at their classmates" — to join in on the riot. Gladwell writes, "In the day of [the Columbine shooters], we could try to console ourselves with the thought that there was nothing we could do, that no law or intervention or restrictions on guns could make a difference in the face of someone so evil. But the riot has now engulfed the boys who were once content to play with chemistry sets in the basement. The problem is not that there is an endless supply of deeply disturbed young men who are willing to contemplate horrific acts. It's worse. It's that young men no longer need to be deeply disturbed to contemplate horrific acts."

That theory isn't just conjecture on Gladwell's part. In an article written by Mark Follman and Becca Andrews titled *How Columbine Spawned Dozens of Copycats*, Follman and Andrews observed that in at least 14 cases, "Columbine copycats aimed to attack on the anniversary of the original massacre. Individuals in 13 cases indicated that their goal was to outdo the Columbine body count. In at least 10 cases, the suspects and attackers referred to the pair who struck in 1999, [...] as heroes, idols, martyrs or God. And at least three plotters made pilgrimages to Columbine High School from other states."

When Did Fame Become a Career Choice?

The threshold model isn't the only theory that explains why active shootings are on the rise, or why each subsequent mass shooter seems desperate to outdo his predecessors. In other words, it isn't enough for new mass shooters to say, "me too." Instead, their planning and actions point to an attempt to beat their predecessors in body count, as though it's a competition. And in a way, it is. A competition to be the most talked about, the most reviled and the most famous. That preoccupation with fame isn't something that's unique to mass shooters; it is part of a measurable societal shift among teens and preteens documented by Dr. Yalda Uhls, a child development researcher at UCLA. In a multiyear study, Dr. Uhls interviewed teens and preteens, asking them to rank the values that they found most important. Prior to 2007, Dr. Uhls found "community" and "family" near the top of the list. But by 2007, those values had dropped on the scale, and "fame" had moved into the No. 1 position. Two or three generations ago, when asked what they wanted to be when they grew up, children would answer with the usual responses of wanting to be an astronaut, a sports star, a doctor or the president. In today's generation, the top "career choice" that kids want to shoot for is "fame." In the Kardashian era in which we find ourselves, when people are famous for simply being famous, the idea that hard work is required to achieve life's goals (or to achieve actual fame rather than infamy) is losing the battle when compared to the dream of instant stardom. When every preteen and teenager in America can name a dozen millennials who have skipped college and made millions through nothing more than their number of Instagram or YouTube followers, the thought of slogging through eight years of medical school to achieve guaranteed success in life may have lost its luster. When those dreams of instant stardom fade (or when dreams of love or success on the sports field fade) boys and sometimes girls)who carry other risk factors may choose to find fame another way. Dr. Reid Meloy summarizes this theory by stating, "Their acts result in notoriety, a sick celebrity status, and that's a powerful allure for young people who, in some cases, haven't really found a place to belong in the real world."

The shooter who killed nine at Umpqua Community College was apparently susceptible to the allure of instant fame. Prior to his attack, Chris Harper-Mercer posted online that he admired the infamy of Vester Lee Flanagan, who shot and killed reporter Alison Parker and photojournalist Adam Ward, employees of CBS affiliate WDBJ in Roanoke, Virginia in 2015. Harper-Mercer wrote, "A man who was known by no one, is now known by everyone. His face splashed across every screen, his name across the lips of every person on the planet, all in the course of one day. Seems the more people you kill, the more you're in the limelight."

While society as a whole is shifting to elevate fame over sacrifice, service and hard work, parents have an opportunity to counteract that pull. We'll discuss those ideas in Part Two.

SNAPSHOT

Since the Columbine shooting in 1999, there have been a total of 165 events that the FBI has categorized as "active shooting events." As I mentioned, the FBI doesn't count events that were a result of some other crime being committed, so if you've seen data from another source, you may have seen a number larger or smaller than 165 events. Of those 165 events, 48 of them would fall into the smaller category of "mass shootings," which, by the FBI's definition, is an event where four or more people were fatally shot during an active shooting event. Those mass shootings resulted in 448 people killed (not including the shooter) and another 369 wounded. Interestingly, the dead to wounded ratio during mass shootings is the opposite of what the American military has seen in every military conflict since the Revolutionary War. For example, during the war in Iraq, 10 soldiers died for every 73 wounded (a ratio of 1:7.3). During mass shootings, 10 people will die for every eight wounded (a ratio of 1.2:1). Contributing factors to this high ratio of dead to wounded can include: the high number of rounds fired into each victim; the close contact range of the shooter to his victims; and delayed medical treatment while EMS professionals wait to be cleared for entry. We'll explore each of those contributing factors in greater detail.

Not surprisingly, 95 percent of the shooters were male, the average age being 34.

165

Active Shooter Events have occurred in the U.S. since Columbine.

3   45

48

ASEs met the FBI's definition of a "mass shooting" (4 or more fatalities).

448

People were killed in mass shootings (not including the shooter).

369

People were wounded in mass shootings.

Source: Dr. Pete Blair, Hunter Martaindale and Terry Nichols, *Active Shooter Events from 2000 to 2013.*

LOCATIONS

While two of the most deadly ASEs in the United States occurred at schools (Sandy Hook Elementary and Virginia Tech), school shootings account for just 24 percent of all ASEs with shootings at businesses occurring at almost double that frequency. Shootings on government property accounted for 10 percent of the total, with shootings at houses of worship accounting for about 4 percent of the total. It's also helpful to break down the number of shootings that have occurred at businesses — of the 73 ASEs that have occurred at businesses, almost 70 percent of those occurred at businesses open to the public, including malls. If this chart tells us anything, it's that no place is immune from the scourge of mass shooters — military bases, churches, colleges and universities, elementary schools, offices, malls and night clubs. No place is immune.

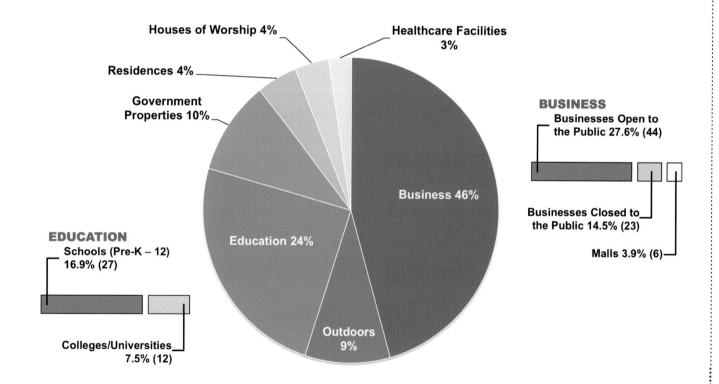

Source: Dr. Pete Blair, Hunter Martaindale, and Terry Nichols, *Active Shooter Events from 2000 to 2013.*

EMANUEL A.M.E. CHURCH

Flowers are stacked at a makeshift memorial at the entrance to the Emanuel African Methodist Episcopal Church in Charleston, South Carolina. Police reports indicate that on June 17, 2015, nine people were killed by a gunman, including the senior pastor, state senator Clementa Pinckney. The morning after the attack, police made an arrest. During the murderer's interrogation, he admitted that he committed the shooting in hopes of igniting a race war.

EVENT RESOLUTION

On the charts shown below and on the opposite page, I've detailed the different ways that these events have ended. The chart below combines all outcomes, regardless of whether the event ended before or after the arrival of police on the scene, while the flowchart on the opposite page provides a breakdown of event resolution by when the event ended. Disturbingly, the chart on this page shows that 40 percent of active shooters commit suicide in place, while only 4 percent surrender to police. But let me add something that you don't see on this chart.

While 40 percent of all active shooters commit suicide in place, 70 percent of school shooters take their own life. This indicates that school shooters in particular do not have an escape plan because they do not intend to escape. When 10 times as many shooters choose to kill themselves rather than surrender, it's clear that these shooters cannot be reasoned with. They will not listen to pleas of mercy, and they will certainly not spare the life of any man, woman or child, regardless of how old or how young. As disturbing, the flowchart on the opposite page shows that in more than 55 percent of the cases (90 events), the event was over before the police arrived on the scene. That indicates that these events start

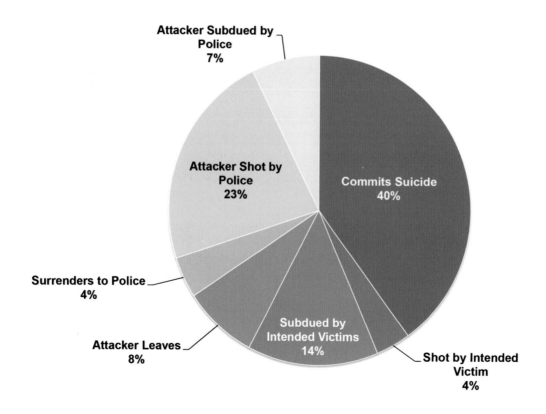

Attacker Subdued by Police 7%

Attacker Shot by Police 23%

Commits Suicide 40%

Surrenders to Police 4%

Attacker Leaves 8%

Subdued by Intended Victims 14%

Shot by Intended Victim 4%

Source: Dr. Pete Blair, Hunter Martaindale, and Terry Nichols, *Active Shooter Events from 2000 to 2013.*

and end quickly, and that the outcome may be more dependent upon the action (or inaction) of the potential victims than the action of the police when they arrive. Speaking of victim action, the data in these charts also shows some good news, revealing that in 14 percent of the cases (23 events), the shooter was subdued by his intended victims prior to police arrival. In 4 percent of the cases (six events), the attacker was actually shot by his intended victims. We'll spend plenty of time talking more about that subject in Part Two.

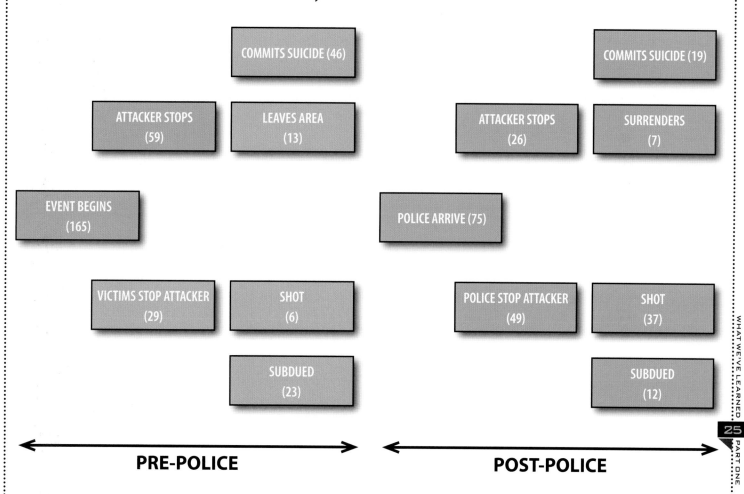

PRE-POLICE

POST-POLICE

■ *The flowchart above shows the same data on the opposite page in a different layout, broken down by whether the event was resolved prior to police arriving or after the police arrived on the scene. Of the 165 active shooting events, 90 events ended before the police arrived, with 75 events ending after the police arrived. Of the attackers who committed suicide in place, nearly two-thirds commit suicide before the police arrived.*

Source: Dr. Pete Blair, Hunter Martaindale and Terry Nichols, *Active Shooter Events from 2000 to 2013.*

Law enforcement prepares to make entry at Umpqua Community College to stop a mass shooter, a 26-year-old enrolled at UCC. Before committing suicide as police closed in, the attacker fatally shot an assistant professor and eight students and wounded nine others. The following is a timeline released by Douglas County Sheriff John Hanlin: The first 911 call came in at 10:38 a.m. on October 1. Roseburg Police officers and medical were notified. Sheriff Hanlin noted that police officers were 5 miles away from the campus. One minute later, at 10:39, dispatch sent out an update stating the shooter was in the science building. At 10:40, the UCC campus was put into lockdown. One minute later, shots were reported coming from the Snyder Building. Oregon State Police received reports of an active shooter at 10:42. At 10:44, six minutes after the first 911 call, the first two Roseburg Police officers arrive, as well as one OSP trooper. Officers report exchanging shots with the suspect at 10:46. "Suspect down" comes over the radio at 10:48, 10 minutes after the first 911 call was received.

POLICE RESPONSE TIME

The last data point that we'll look at is the average response time for law enforcement to arrive on the scene of these active shootings, which is often commendable. For example, the police arrived outside the Aurora theater shooting an amazing 90 seconds after the first 911 calls came in. But arriving on the scene is one thing; entering the building to stop the shooter is another. While the Aurora police were on-scene 90 seconds after the first 911 calls, those calls weren't made until two minutes into the attack, and the police didn't apprehend Holmes until nine minutes after the shooting began. At Umpqua Community College (profiled on the opposite page) the police arrived on the scene six minutes after the first 911 calls. In San Bernardino, the police arrived on the scene four minutes after the shooting began, which happens to be the national average for these events. Four minutes on average for the police to arrive on scene, after 911 has been called. This isn't a knock on the police. It's the reality of what happens when the only good guys with guns are coming from miles away and require at least several minutes to formulate a plan once arriving on-scene.

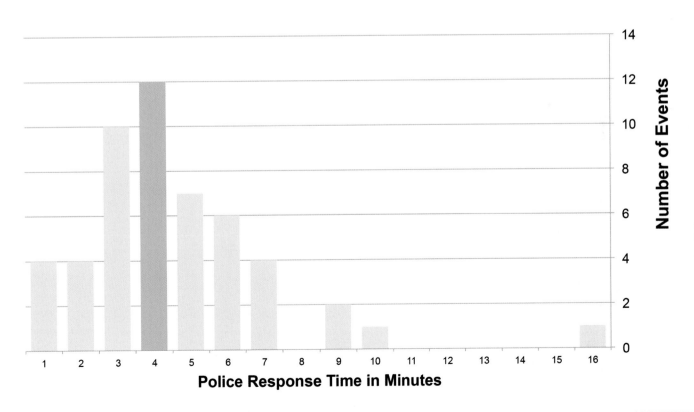

Source: Dr. Pete Blair, Hunter Martaindale and Terry Nichols, *Active Shooter Events from 2000 to 2013.*

WILL REDUCING MAGAZINE CAPACITY WORK?

NOW THAT WE HAVE A COMMON SET OF DEFINITIONS AND DATA TO WORK WITH, we'll begin to analyze a number of factors to determine what effect those factors have on the final outcome, either positively or negatively. The first factors that we'll analyze will be to determine whether a reduction in magazine capacity or banning AR-15s or any other class of firearm will reduce or has reduced the carnage caused by these mass shooters. We'll start by using data from each of the 48 mass shootings since Columbine to determine whether magazine capacities greater than five or 10 rounds have had a major effect, a minor effect or no effect on the outcome at those attacks.

The argument that "high capacity" magazines are partially (or mostly) to blame for mass shootings isn't a new one, but it reached a fever pitch in the aftermath of Sandy Hook, when the states of Connecticut, New York and Colorado all enacted new limits on magazine capacity.

The argument put forward by these states was based upon the belief that it was a high rate of fire enabled by magazine capacities of 30 rounds or more that allowed these monsters to murder a large number of victims in a short period of time. The theory was that by reducing magazine capacities by up to two-thirds, the number of victims would be greatly reduced at future mass shootings. This theory wasn't one that gun-control advocates latched onto halfheartedly. It was the centerpiece of their proposals on how to reduce or eliminate future mass shootings.

> *"Semiautomatic firearms with the capacity to accept detachable high-capacity ammunition magazines are the single lethal thread that runs through the vast majority of mass shootings in the United States. High-capacity ammunition magazines help put the 'mass' in mass shooting."*
> *Josh Sugarmann,*
> *Director of the*
> *Violence Policy Center*

A couple commonly held opinions were expressed by former New York Rep. Carolyn McCarthy and by Josh Sugarmann, the director of the Violence Policy Center.

McCarthy said, "There's one simple, common thread in every single mass shooting in recent history: the use of high-capacity magazines in order to kill as many people as possible in the shortest amount of time. Taking high-capacity magazines off the shelves for civilians would present a major obstacle for the next murderer trying to equip to kill large numbers of people. It can save lives in America."

Sugarmann agreed with that sentiment when he said, "Semiautomatic firearms with the capacity to accept detachable high-capacity ammunition magazines are the single lethal thread that runs through the vast majority of mass shootings in the United States. High-capacity ammunition magazines help put the 'mass' in mass shooting."

So that begs the question: exactly how many rounds can be fired per minute when using magazine capacities of five rounds, 10 rounds or 30 rounds, and would a lower round capacity have affected the outcome at any mass shooting? In other words, are McCarthy and Sugarmann right?

To answer the first half of that question, let's look at the actual rates of fire attainable with three different sizes of magazine. The table on the opposite page shows how many rounds can be fired per minute using a moderate rate of fire of two rounds per second and a moderate magazine change rate of three seconds. I'll add that someone with practice would be able to fire at about twice this rate. As you can see, the table shows that reducing a magazine capacity by two-thirds doesn't reduce the rate of fire by two-thirds, of course. It simply means that more magazine changes are required per minute. The actual reduction in rate of fire when going from a 30-round magazine to a 10-round magazine is about 25 percent. The math is simple — with a 30-round magazine and a moderate rate of fire of two rounds per second, a shooter would

MAGAZINE CAPACITY	RELOADS REQUIRED PER MINUTE	ROUNDS PER MINUTE
5 Rounds	11	55
10 Rounds	7.5	75
30 Rounds	3.3	100

be able to sustain a rate of fire of about 100 rounds per minute. Using 10-round magazines, that same shooter would be able to sustain a rate of fire of about 75 rounds per minute. The decrease in rate of fire would occur because the shooter would need to go from about 3.3 magazine changes per minute to about 7 magazine changes per minute. If dropping to 5-round magazines, that same shooter would be able to fire 55 rounds per minute. Now, just to confirm for you that I'm not manipulating these numbers to make any particular case, you can mimic this test yourself by pressing your index finger twice per second, as though you were shooting a gun. My assumption is that you'll recognize pretty easily that you can press your finger *much* faster than twice per second. So we could easily double the rates of fire shown on

"There's one simple, common thread in every single mass shooting in recent history: the use of high-capacity magazines in order to kill as many people as possible in the shortest amount of time. Taking high-capacity magazines off the shelves for civilians would present a major obstacle for the next murderer trying to equip to kill large numbers of people. It can save lives in America."
Former New York Rep. Carolyn McCarthy

the table. But in a moment, you'll see why I'm satisfied with the data, as we attempt to answer the second half of the question posed earlier, which is: Would a lower magazine capacity have affected the outcome at any mass shooting? In other words, if former Rep. McCarthy and Sugarmann are correct, we should find clear and convincing evidence that mass shooters are attaining a rate of fire of 100 rounds per minute or more. Otherwise, to paraphrase Sugarmann, there would be no "mass" in mass shootings. Said another way, the "magazine" argument believes that if the rate of fire of these shooters can be reduced to the limits imposed by 5- or 10-round magazines, the number of victims at mass shootings would be significantly reduced. But before we answer that question, let's look at these rates of fire visually, so we can figure out together whether a reduction in magazine size would have an effect on the rates of fire during mass shootings.

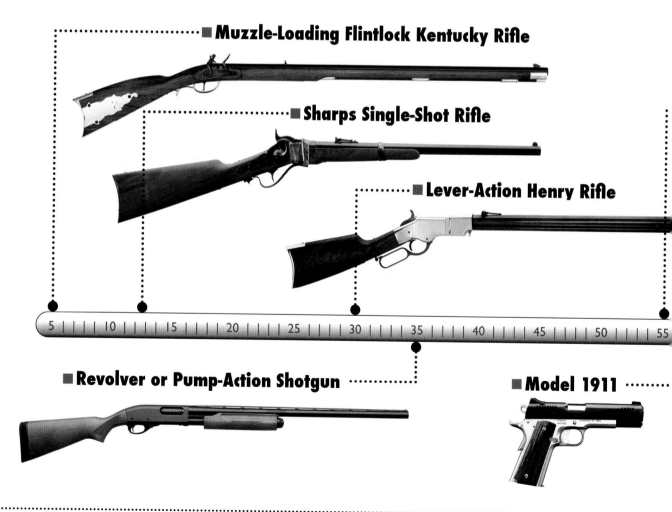

■ **Muzzle-Loading Flintlock Kentucky Rifle**

■ **Sharps Single-Shot Rifle**

■ **Lever-Action Henry Rifle**

5 | | | 10 | | | 15 | | | 20 | | | 25 | | | 30 | | | 35 | | | 40 | | | 45 | | | 50 | | | 55

■ **Revolver or Pump-Action Shotgun**

■ **Model 1911**

On the linear scale shown below, I've placed the three rates of fire possible when using 5, 10 or 30-round magazines on the right side of the scale. To summarize the point I made earlier, if we were to ban all 30-round magazines and replace them with 10-round magazines, we'd be moving the theoretical maximum rate of fire from 100 rounds per minute to 75 rounds per minute, which is a reduction of 25 percent. My guess is that when state legislatures and governors across the country debated magazine capacity in the aftermath of Sandy Hook, they probably thought that they'd get more than a 25 percent reduction in rate of fire, but the math is difficult to dispute.

To give some comparative rates of fire, I'm going to jump back more than 240 years to take a look at what rates of fire used to be. Let's start with the muzzle-loading Kentucky rifle, which was the preferred rifle of the American patriots during the Revolutionary

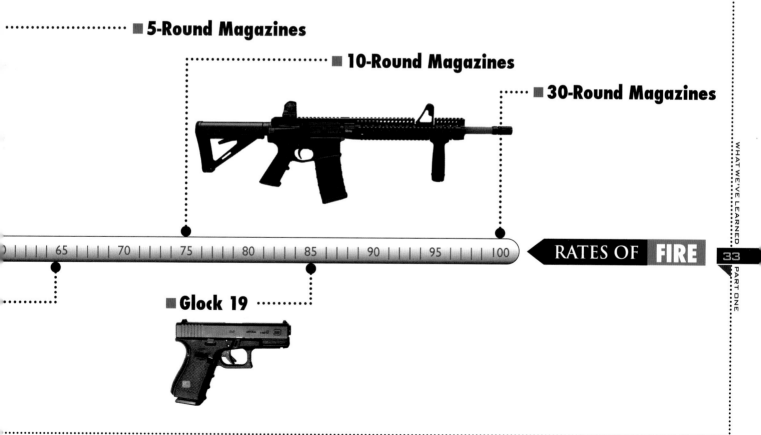

■ 5-Round Magazines

■ 10-Round Magazines

■ 30-Round Magazines

65 | | | | 70 | | | | 75 | | | | 80 | | | | 85 | | | | 90 | | | | 95 | | | | 100

RATES OF **FIRE**

■ Glock 19

■ The 7th Illinois Volunteer Infantry sporting their Henry rifles, which could sustain a rate of fire of 30 rounds per minute.

War. As a muzzle-loading firearm, the Kentucky rifle took four separate steps to load, but an experienced shooter was able to maintain a rate of fire of about five rounds per minute. I've placed that rifle on the far left side of the scale. As firearm technology advanced, self-contained cartridges were developed, which led to the development of the Sharps single-shot rifle in 1848. Loading one round at a time, the Sharps more than doubled rates of fire, up to an average rate of 12 rounds fired per minute. Fast forward to the Civil War, and the height of firearms technology was the lever-action Henry rifle (shown in the photo above of the Illinois 7th Infantry), which enabled a sustained rate of fire of about

30 rounds per minute. If you've ever watched the movie *Dances with Wolves*, that was a Henry rifle that Kevin Costner used in the famous scene where he dropped a charging buffalo moments before it ran over a young Native American.

Lastly, I'm going to drop in the rates of fire for several other firearm types. Five-shot revolvers and five-shot pump action shotguns are able to sustain a rate of fire of about 35 rounds per minute, which is a bit slower than semi-automatics using five-round magazines since they take slightly longer to reload. I've also included a model 1911 pistol which uses a seven-round magazine and can sustain a rate of fire of about 65 rounds per minute.

And finally, the Glock 19 uses a magazine size of 15 rounds, which results in a rate of fire of about 85 rounds per minute. In a moment, I'll explain the purpose of this scale, which will be used to answer the second question posed earlier: "Would a lower magazine capacity have affected the outcome at any mass shooting?"

The Connecticut Legislature and governor certainly believed the answer was a resounding "Yes," believing

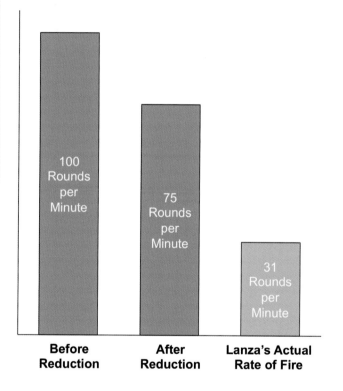

■ By reducing the maximum magazine capacity in Connecticut from 30 rounds to 10 rounds, the Connecticut Legislature and governor effectively reduced the theoretical maximum rate of fire from 100 rounds per minute to 75 rounds per minute. But here's the problem. The actual rate of fire used by Sandy Hook shooter was just 31 rounds per minute, or less than half the new limit just imposed. Had this law been in place before the Sandy Hook shooting, nothing would have changed.

magazine capacity was mostly to blame for the massacre at Sandy Hook. In the months following the shooting, they effectively told the Sandy Hook parents that their swift and decisive action of reducing the legal magazine capacity in Connecticut from 30 to 10 (plus a renewed ban on semi-automatic rifles that could accept these magazines) would ensure that such a massacre would never occur again. So let's see what effect that reduction had in Connecticut. As you can see on the chart shown on the left, before the magazine reduction in Connecticut, the theoretical maximum rate of fire was about 100 rounds per minute. After the magazine reduction, the new theoretical rate of fire was 75 rounds per minute. Not much of a reduction, but a reduction nonetheless. Here's the problem: The *actual* rate of fire used by the Sanday Hook attacker was just 31 rounds per minute, or one round every two seconds. In other words, he fired at a rate less than *half* of the new limit that Connecticut just imposed. Obviously, a high rate of fire didn't matter to him, and he didn't need to shoot quickly to commit his horrible crime.

The magazine argument crumbles even further when looking at the rates of fire of other mass shooters, including the 10 worst shootings as shown on the table on the following page. (At the time I compiled this data, no information has been released about the number of rounds fired by the Orlando shooter). These shooters all fired at a rate *significantly* less than the new limit established in Connecticut, which is one of the lowest in the nation. A high rate of fire apparently didn't matter to any of these shooters.

Let's state these facts with a little perspective: The Newtown shooter fired at a rate of fire no faster than

MASS SHOOTER RATES OF FIRE

LOCATION	NUMBER KILLED	ROUNDS FIRED	EVENT DURATION	ROUNDS FIRED PER MINUTE
Virginia Tech	30[1]	174	11 minutes	15
Sandy Hook	26	154	5 - 9 minutes[2]	15 - 31
San Bernardino	14	65 - 75	5 minutes	7 - 14[3]
Fort Hood	13	214	10 minutes	21
Binghampton	13	99	4 minutes	25
Columbine	13	188	47 minutes	4
Aurora	12	70	5 - 9 minutes	8 - 14[4]
Umpqua	9	85[5]	9 minutes	9
Charleston	9	74	7 minutes	11
Red Lake	9	45	9 minutes	5

[1]The assailant killed a total of 32 people at Virginia Tech in two separate attacks. For purposes of calculating his rate of fire, only the second attack is included on this table where a total of 30 people were killed.

[2]Police records indicate that Lanza shot his way into Sandy Hook Elementary at 9:35 a.m., and at 9:40 a.m. (five minutes after the shooting began) the last shot was heard, which is believed to be Lanza taking his own life. Police entered the school four minutes later, at 9:44 a.m. (9 minutes after the shooting began).

[3]Since the San Bernardino shooting involved two shooters, the calculation of rounds fired per minute shows a spread of 7 – 14 rounds fired per minute. If one shooter was responsible for all rounds fired, the rate would be approximately 14 rounds fired per minute. If both shooters fired an equal number of rounds, their individual rates would be approximately seven rounds fired per minute, or one round every 8.5 seconds.

[4]The timeline of the Aurora Theater shooting indicates that Holmes opened fire at 12:37, the first 911 call was received at 12:39 (two minutes after the shooting began), the first police arrived on the scene at 12:41 (four minutes after the shooting began), police began to surround the theater by 12:42 as witnesses report that there is still "someone actively shooting" inside (five minutes after the shooting began) and Holmes is apprehended outside the back of the theater at 12:46 (nine minutes after the shooting began).

[5]This is a calculated estimate based upon the handgun model used and the number of magazines in Harper-Mercer's possession. The actual number of rounds fired may be far less.

the 150-year-old lever-action Henry rifle, popular among Union soldiers in the Civil War, even though he had ten 30-round magazines and an AR-15. The Fort Hood shooter was a third slower than that, while the Virginia Tech attacker was 50 percent slower. Even the San Bernardino shooters who carried AR-15s and 30-round magazines fired at a rate no faster than one round every 3.3 seconds, which is 40 percent *slower* than the lever-action Henry. The Aurora, Colorado, theater assailant fired at a rate no faster than the 170-year-old, single-shot Sharps rifle, developed 13 years before the Civil War began, even though he had a 100-round magazine. Keep in mind, the Sharps rifle has a capacity of one round, or 99 rounds fewer than the Aurora shooter had in his magazine. Finally, the Red Lake shooter as well as the Columbine shooters fired at a rate of fire no faster than the 240-year-old, muzzle-loading flintlock Kentucky rifle, favored by the American patriots in the Revolutionary War.

Now let's summarize those actual rates of fire back onto the linear scale we created earlier. Remember, if McCarthy and Sugarmann are correct, we should see the actual rates of fire for all mass shooters clustered at the upper end of the scale. But instead, every one of them is clustered at the lower end of the scale, all firing at a rate no faster than the 150-year-old lever-action Henry rifle. Most were dramatically slower than that, regardless of the choice of firearm type or magazine size.

This isn't fuzzy math I'm using. For example, it is well documented that the San Bernardino shooters fired 65 to 75 rounds during their five-minute attack. If just one of the shooters fired all of the rounds, their rate of fire

The Newtown shooter fired at a rate of fire no faster than the 150-year-old, lever-action Henry rifle, popular among Union soldiers in the Civil War, even though he had ten, 30-round magazines and an AR-15. The Fort Hood shooter was a third slower than that, while the Virginia Tech attacker was 50 percent slower.

would still just be 14 rounds per minute, or one round fired every 4 seconds. If both shooters fired an equal number of rounds, their individual rates would be no higher than seven rounds per minute, or one round every 8 seconds. Now, you could argue that perhaps the shooters in every one of these cases were simply inexperienced and unable to press their trigger finger faster than once every 4 to 8 seconds. But that's actually a pretty silly argument, considering how easy it is to test that theory by pressing your finger faster than twice per second while you sit and read this book. In the case of the San Bernardino shooters, there is also

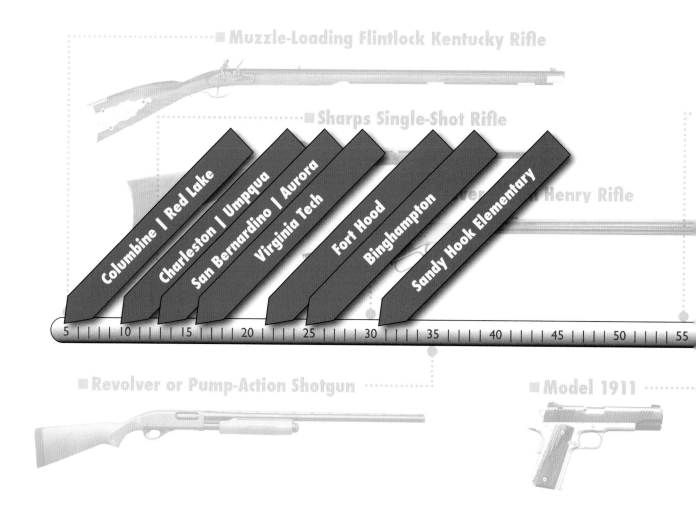

ample evidence that the shooters practiced frequently at a local range. A simpler explanation on why these shooters have such a low rate of fire, and the one that makes the most sense, is that when these shooters have their victims held captive in an enclosed area and they are the only ones with the guns, they simply don't *need*

to press the trigger faster than once every four to eight seconds. When you're firing at that pace, magazine size simply doesn't matter.

So let's summarize. The premise that magazine capacity has anything to do with the number of dead at any mass shooting seems to be completely

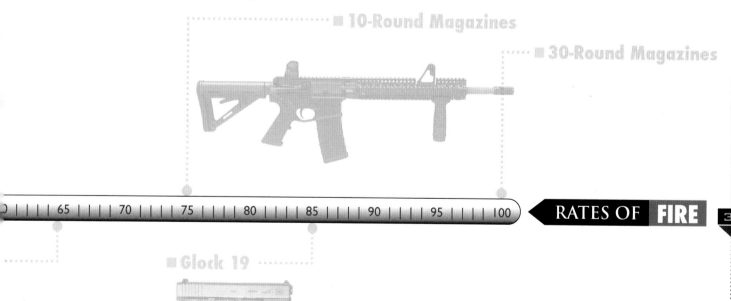

RATES OF **FIRE**

Sandy Hook

26 DEAD

The murderer who entered Sandy Hook Elementary with ten 30-round magazines didn't even take advantage of the full capacity before reloading. Three magazines were unused, and four others were left with 10, 11, 13 and 14 rounds remaining.

ROUNDS REMAINING AFTER SHOOTING

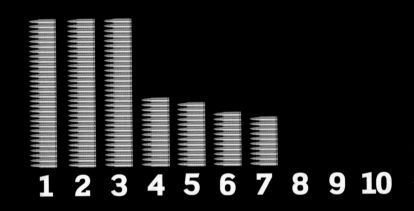

1 2 3 4 5 6 7 8 9 10

without merit. Even the Aurora theater perpetrator, who had a 100-round magazine, used a rate of fire no faster than one round every four to seven seconds, which is no faster than a single-shot rifle. Rapid fire didn't matter to him.

The murderer who entered Sandy Hook Elementary with ten 30-round magazines didn't even take advantage of the full capacity before reloading. Three magazines were unused and four others were left with 10, 11, 13 and 14 rounds remaining. He didn't need a high rate of fire *or* the extra rounds.

Neither did the Virginia Tech shooter. Although he had ten 15-round magazines with him, he filled six of them with just 10 rounds and four with just 11 rounds. The gunman had seven other 10-round magazines for a total of 17 magazines loaded with 174 rounds. That's an average of 10.2 rounds per magazine, which is just a hair above the new limit imposed by Connecticut. He emptied every one of his 17 magazines by firing one round every four seconds, which isn't rapid fire by anyone's

Virginia Tech

32 DEAD

In the official report of the Virginia Tech shooting commissioned by the Virginia governor, the authoring panel commented, "Having the ammunition in large capacity magazines facilitated Cho's killing spree." There's just one problem with that conclusion.

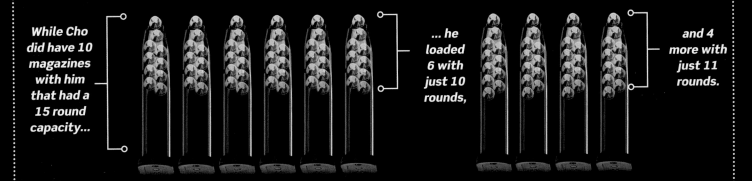

While Cho did have 10 magazines with him that had a 15 round capacity...

... he loaded 6 with just 10 rounds,

and 4 more with just 11 rounds.

Cho had seven other 10-round magazines for a total of 17 magazines loaded with 174 rounds, or an average of 10.2 rounds per magazine. The panel was wrong. If Cho had been limited to magazines with a maximum capacity of 10 rounds, nothing would have changed.

definition, yet 30 people died in Norris Hall.

Now, what's amazing about that last fact is that in the official report of the Virginia Tech shooting commissioned by the Virginia governor, the authoring panel considered whether the expired federal Assault Weapons Act of 1994 that banned 15-round magazines and limited magazine capacity to 10 rounds would have made a difference in the Virginia Tech shooting had the Act still been in force. Apparently, they *did* think it would have made a difference. In the key findings section, the

panel commented, "Having the ammunition in large capacity magazines facilitated [the] killing spree." The panel apparently never did the math to conclude that even though Cho carried a number of 15-round magazines, he loaded them as though they were 10-round magazines. This belief that magazine capacity has anything to do with the number of dead at these mass shootings seems to so permeate this debate that logic and even basic mathematics seem to get thrown out the window.

Finally, the San Bernardino shooters, who each

carried AR-15s and multiple 30-round magazines, didn't even top the rate of fire of the single-shot Sharps rifle. With 70 defenseless people in an enclosed room, rapid fire would just mean misses.

In fact, of the 48 mass shootings where data has been made publicly available on both the number of rounds fired and the duration of the event, just one event stands out from the rest, and you have to go two-thirds of the way down the list to number 30 until you can find it. In the 2011 shooting in Tucson, Arizona, where U.S. Rep. Gabby Giffords was critically injured, the shooter fired 31 rounds in about 15 seconds from a single, 33-round magazine before he was tackled by bystanders as he attempted to reload. If the attacker had been using 10-round magazines, he could have fired the same number of rounds in about 21 seconds.

Of course, if he had been using 10-round magazines, it's unknown whether the bystanders could have moved fast enough to stop him after his first or second reload or whether the results would have been the same. Even in this case, the magazine argument isn't clear-cut, and it would be speculation to claim that the number of victims would have been cut by 1/3 or 2/3 if Loughner had been using three 10-round magazines instead of a single 33-round magazine. We'll actually talk a bit more about this event when we discuss how victim response affects the outcome.

Using nothing more than second-grade math, the "magazine argument" crumbles. It is a false lead that has consumed far too many years and has come at the expense of real solutions.

Let me add a personal note here. As I started this research into rates of fire and whether magazine capacity had any influence on the outcome at mass shootings, I was fully prepared to accept whatever result my analysis told me. If I had discovered that the availability of AR-15s and 30-round magazines was tipping the scale in favor of mass shooters, I would have published those results. As a parent, my responsibility to my sons would certainly have outweighed any loyalty I have to the industry where I make my living, and I would have taken the lumps if I felt it necessary to argue in favor of a magazine reduction. But the data clearly indicated that magazine capacity or firearm type had nothing to do with the outcome at event after event. When those facts became apparent, I didn't feel any relief for my industry. Instead, I became angry that years have been wasted debating this red herring. Think about the resources that the average U.S. member of congress and senator has at his or her disposal. If they truly wanted to uncover the factors that affect these mass shootings, they could have uncovered this same data in days rather than the months that it took me. If I can gather this data and draw these conclusions sitting at my kitchen table, why couldn't the hundreds of state and federal representatives who argued in favor of a magazine reduction have done the same thing with the millions of dollars at their disposal? When I hear the phrase, "It's a common-sense solution," I now understand that

that's code for, "I haven't done a bit of research on this topic and I'm going to go with the easy answer." I'd say the time is up for easy answers.

Unintended Consequences

In addition to redirecting our attention from solutions that actually stand a chance of saving lives, knee-jerk reactions such as Connecticut's, Colorado's and New York's to reduce the maximum magazine capacity to 10 rounds can sometimes lead to unintended consequences.

For example, as every experienced shooter knows, the larger the magazine capacity, the higher the rate of malfunction. A 100-round magazine will malfunction more frequently than a 30-round magazine, and a 30-round magazine will malfunction more frequently than a 10-round magazine. The reason for this has to do with the length of the spring pushing the rounds through the magazine. The longer the spring, the greater the pressure on the initial rounds, resulting in a higher probability of a double-feed or of the magazine's follower becoming misaligned and locking in place, rendering the magazine temporarily useless. Let's look at a couple of examples.

The Aurora, Colorado, theater gunman brought one single AR-15 magazine with him, and it held 100 rounds. Not only did that make his firearm incredibly heavy and unwieldy, the magazine failed completely after approximately 45 rounds, and his incredibly slow rate of fire (one round every four to seven seconds, no faster than a single-shot rifle) would indicate that he most likely was fighting misfeeds right up until the point that the magazine

■ *Based upon statements from the children and evidence at the scene, it appears Lanza's AR-15 malfunctioned, and he was forced to pause to clear the malfunction. Evidence of a malfunction included unshot rounds found on the floor, which would be typical of a double-feed (when two rounds try to feed into the chamber at the same time). To clear a double-feed, the shooter must remove the magazine and retract the bolt to clear the action — causing two or more rounds to drop to the floor — before reinserting the magazine and releasing the bolt. Double-feed failures are common when using 30-round magazines that have been filled to capacity, as his were.*

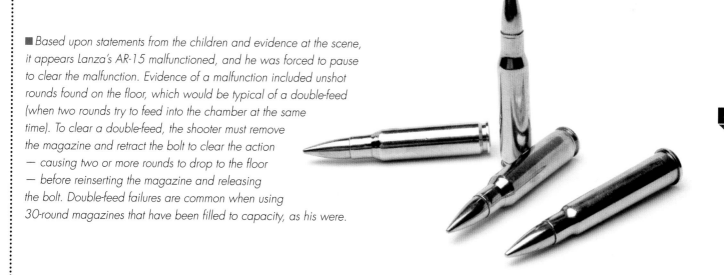

failed completely. Had he been using 10-round magazines, it's unlikely that any failure would have occurred, and his rate of fire could have been much higher.

Another example: Police reports indicate that at one point during his shooting spree, the Sandy Hook attacker paused, which allowed nine children to flee a classroom. Based upon statements from the children and evidence at the scene, it appears as though his AR-15 malfunctioned, and he was forced to pause to clear the malfunction. Evidence of a malfunction included unshot rounds found on the floor, which would be typical of a double-feed (when two rounds try to feed into the chamber at the same time). To clear a double-feed, the shooter must remove the magazine, retract the bolt to clear the action — causing two or more rounds to drop to the floor — before reinserting the magazine and releasing the bolt. Double-feed failures are common when using 30-round magazines that have been filled to capacity, as his were. These malfunctions are far less common in 10-round magazines because of the shorter springs and lower spring pressure on the initial rounds. Had he been using 10-round magazines, a double-feed or other failure would have been far less likely.

Now, I'm not suggesting that future victims of mass shootings will be safer if the shooter chooses to use 100-round or 30-round magazines rather than 10-round magazines, but what I am suggesting is that when a politician who knows absolutely nothing about firearms attempts to make firearms policy, he or she shouldn't be surprised when their actions don't have the desired effect. Take a look at the quote below from Colorado State Rep. Diana DeGette. She clearly

"I will tell you these are ammunition, they're bullets, so the people who have those now, they're going to shoot them. So if you ban them in the future, the number of these high-capacity magazines is going to decrease dramatically over time, because the bullets will have been shot and there won't be any more available."

Diana DeGette (D)
Colorado State Rep.

had no idea what magazines even are since she assumes they're a one-time use product, yet she argued vehemently to ban 30-round magazines. Forget for a moment that she was arguing in favor of banning a product which was currently legal. The greater issue here is that she and dozens of other Colorado state representatives and senators said with their arguments and their votes, "We have the solution to put an end to mass shootings." Yet, as shown, the arguments were so far from a real solution that they might as well have done nothing. In fact, those efforts did *worse* than nothing. Instead, the "solutions" lulled far too many people into believing that a simple answer had been found, and nothing could be further from the truth.

Those arguing in favor of a magazine reduction have also suggested that by reducing the maximum capacity of magazines to 10 rounds, it would also reduce the total amount of ammunition that these shooters would bring with them, thereby lowering the casualty rate. That suggestion can only be described as foolish for two reasons. One, if a shooter was truly limited in ammunition capacity by a smaller magazine size, he or she could simply carry more magazines. And two, at every mass shooting profiled here, shooters have run out of victims before they've run out of ammunition.

At Sandy Hook, even if the assailant had brought ten 10-round magazines with him instead of ten 30-round magazines, that would still have left four rounds per victim. At Virginia Tech, if the gunman had been limited to 10-round magazines, it would have lowered his ammunition count by exactly four rounds. Keep in mind that although he had a number of magazines with a 15-round capacity, the perpetrator loaded six of them with just 10 rounds and four of them with 11 rounds. With just four fewer rounds, he would still have had six rounds per victim murdered in Norris Hall. While I will give the lawmakers and governors that passed legislation reducing magazine capacities in their state the benefit of the doubt that they truly were trying to make a difference, their actions make me envision a hypothetical phone call that might go something like this: "Hello, this is your child's school calling. I have good news and bad news. The bad news is that we have an active shooter in your child's school. The good news is that he only has 10-round magazines." I don't mean to make light of the topic with that hypothetical phone call, but it does bring to light just how ridiculous it is to pretend that a magazine capacity reduction will make any difference at all, either in the outcome or in our fear of these mass murderers.

WOULD BANNING AR-15s OR OTHER FIREARMS WORK?

WHEN A MASS SHOOTER SELECTS AN AR-15 AS his weapon of choice, it's usually referred to as a "high-powered" or a "military style" rifle by the media, implying that it's more powerful (and more deadly) than more commonly available rifles, such as rifles used for hunting deer. Let's find out if that's correct

W

ould banking the AR-15 platform save lives at the next mass shooting? Let's try to answer that question by first understanding how often mass shooters use AR-15s. We'll also discuss exactly what kind of round the AR-15 fires to find out if it really is more powerful than other commonly owned rifles.

So just how often do mass shooters use an AR-15 or similar rifle when they commit their crimes? The answer is not many. FBI data shows that attackers have selected an AR-15-style rifle as their weapon of choice in just 10 of the 48 mass shootings that have occurred since Columbine. More revealing, in seven of those cases, the shooters also brought other firearms with them. So in just three out of 48 events does the question posed on the opposite page matter. Is the AR-15 really a "high-powered" rifle compared to other more commonly available rifles? The answer might just redefine what the media considers a "high-powered" rifle to be.

On the page below, I've shown the round fired by the AR-15 in its actual size, alongside the three most popular deer hunting rounds, also shown in their actual size. Which of the four rounds below do you think is fired by the AR-15? If you guessed one of the three larger rounds on the right, you'd be wrong. The AR-15 round is actually the round on the far left, which is the Remington .223. The three rounds to its right are the three most popular deer-hunting rounds, including the .30-30 Winchester, the .308 Winchester and the .30-06 Springfield, respectively. To give you an even better visual for how the Remington .223 stacks up against those popular hunting rounds, the chart on the opposite page compares each of those rounds on a kinetic energy scale, which is the established metric for measuring a round's "power." As you can see, the AR-15 round isn't just physically smaller, it also falls dramatically below those popular deer-hunting rounds in kinetic energy, and well below the kinetic energy of a 12-gauge 000 buckshot shell. I'll add that a 12-gauge 000 (pronounced "triple-ought") buckshot fires six to eight projectiles, all 45 percent *larger* than the hole made by a single

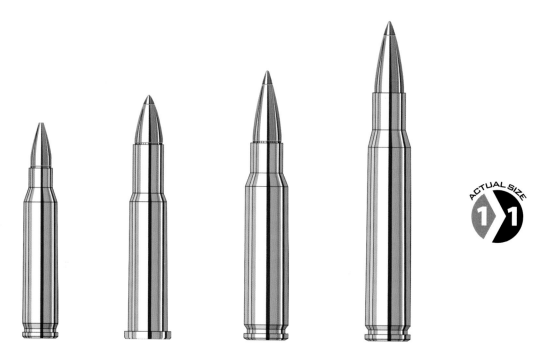

ACTUAL SIZE
1 1

■ *One of the rounds above is the Remington .223 fired by the AR-15, the other three are the most popular deer hunting rounds on the market. Do you know which is which? The answer might just redefine what the media considers to be a "high-powered" rifle.*

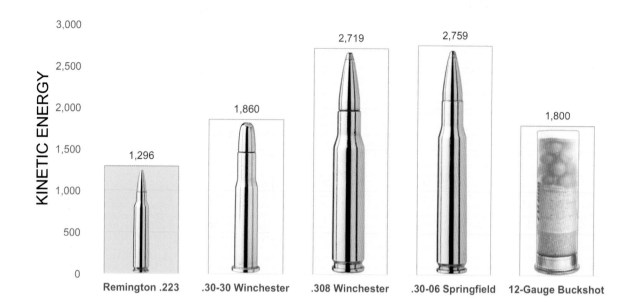

KINETIC ENERGY

3,000					
2,500			2,719	2,759	
2,000		1,860			1,800
1,500	1,296				
1,000					
500					
0	Remington .223	.30-30 Winchester	.308 Winchester	.30-06 Springfield	12-Gauge Buckshot

Remington .223 bullet. Now, I haven't put these illustrations together to make an argument that all ammunition of all types should be banned. Instead, I've shown them as a way of explaining that simply banning one ammunition type or the firearm that shoots that ammunition in the hopes that it will result in less devastation during mass shootings is hopelessly naive.

I hate to be the bearer of bad news, but *any* ammunition type or caliber fired into a human body at close range will have devastating effects. When more than one round is fired into a victim, the devastation is magnified exponentially. As an example, the Virginia Tech shooter killed many of his victims using what would normally be considered a "plinking" round, or a

At Virginia Tech, all of the victims were shot at least three times each. Of the 30 victims killed in Norris Hall, 28 were shot in the head, including one victim with nine bullets fired to the head.

round normally used for shooting squirrels and other small game. The .22 long rifle round is so tiny that most people wouldn't give it serious consideration as a defensive or offensive round — just 100 foot-pounds of energy (less than 1/12 the energy of the Remington .223). Yet when fired into a human body at close range, the results will be as fatal as any of the rounds shown on the previous two pages, or handgun ammunition of any type. At Virginia Tech, all of the victims were shot at least three times each. Of the 30 victims killed in Norris Hall, 28 were shot in the head, including one victim who was shot in the head nine times. The politicians and

6.3 Inches

4.5 Inches

ACTUAL SIZE
1:1

Model: *Walther P22*
Weight: *15 ounces*
Caliber: *.22 long rifle*
Magazine Capacity: *10 rounds*

■ *While gun-control advocates in Washington D.C. were pushing for a renewal of the so-called Assault Weapon Ban (which in part, banned AR-15-style rifles with certain cosmetic features and limited magazine capacity to 10 rounds), at Virginia Tech, defenseless victims were shot in the head with a Walther P22, using 10-round magazines chambered in the diminutive .22 Long Rifle.*

gun-control advocates who are telling you that you'll be safer during a mass shooting if the shooter has 10-round rather than 30-round magazines are the same ones that are implying that you'll be safer if the AR-15 and its so called "high-powered" ammunition were removed from the marketplace. My suggestion is that you not buy into that flawed logic. The solution to ending these crimes does not lie in simply getting rid of any firearm type, any ammunition type or any particular magazine size. While gun-control advocates in Washington D.C. were pushing for a renewal of the so-called Assault Weapon Ban (which in part, banned AR-15 style rifles with certain cosmetic features and limited magazine capacity to 10 rounds), at Virginia Tech, defenseless victims were shot in the head with a Walther P22, using 10-round magazines chambered in the diminutive .22 long rifle as shown below.

■ With just 7 percent of the energy of the AR-15 round and 4 percent of the energy of the 30-06, the .22LR round was still used to devastating effectiveness at Virginia Tech. The shooter proved that when victims are shot at point blank range, caliber does not matter.

The politicians and gun control advocates who are telling you that you'll be safer during a mass shooting if the shooter has 10-round rather than 30-round magazines are the same ones that are implying that you'll be safer if the AR-15 and its so called "high-powered" ammunition were removed from the marketplace. My suggestion is that you not buy into that flawed logic.

DO GUN-FREE ZONES HELP OR HURT?

AFTER EVERY MASS SHOOTING, GUN RIGHTS ORGANIZATIONS POINT THE FINGER at the existence of so-called "gun-free" zones, while gun-control advocates call for even more locations to be declared "gun-free" in an attempt to end mass shootings.

Much has been made of whether mass shooters gravitate toward gun-free zones and if the elimination of schools and other locations as gun-free zones would have a positive or negative effect.

Gun-control advocates have done much to try to dispel the notion that these killers seek out schools or other locations that ban guns. One anti-gun group even tried to dismiss the argument that Fort Hood was a gun-free zone by claiming that the base police who flooded the area and exchanged fire with the shooter proved that Fort Hood was not a gun-free zone after all. But claiming that arriving police means an area isn't a gun-free zone (even though soldiers on base were barred from carrying personal firearms by base policy) is not a valid argument. Instead, let's look at the data.

DEATHS IN GUN-FREE ZONES

Since Columbine, and up to and including the terrorist attacks in San Bernardino and Orlando, 48 mass shootings have occurred with 74 percent of them falling in gun-free zones, where civilians were either disarmed by state law, school policy, federal law or policy, or by private policy. It's worth noting nearly 48 percent of the locations where mass shootings occurred were self-declared gun-free zones, where no law barred civilians from protecting themselves with a firearm. In most cases, it's a university or corporate lawyer who suggests the ban as a way of avoiding liability if a shooting or an accident were to occur. But after looking at this data, those lawyers may want to reevaluate their idea of what "liability" means.

As mentioned, 74 percent of the mass shootings that have occurred since Columbine occurred in gun-free zones, but those shootings were responsible for 85 percent of the deaths, or 379 of 448 murders. That trend in the data clearly indicates that mass shooters actively seek out soft targets while avoiding hardened targets. Signs, school policies, corporate policies, state statutes, glass doors, unlocked doors and unarmed victims do not create hardened targets. Instead what those things create is the perfect environment for these deranged individuals to successfully carry out their plans. If we change the environment, we stand a chance at changing their plans. We'll talk more about that idea in Part Two.

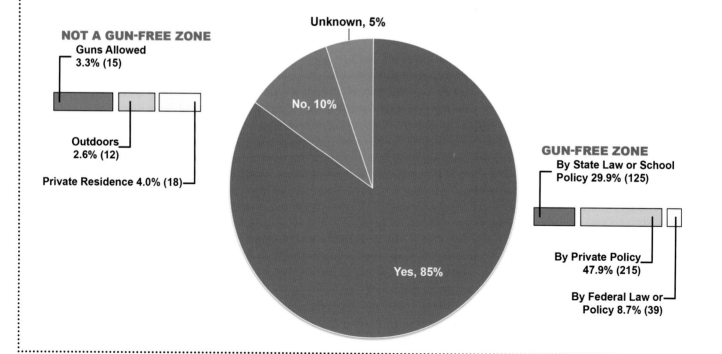

Unknown, 5%

NOT A GUN-FREE ZONE
Guns Allowed
3.3% (15)

Outdoors
2.6% (12)

Private Residence 4.0% (18)

No, 10%

Yes, 85%

GUN-FREE ZONE
By State Law or School Policy 29.9% (125)

By Private Policy
47.9% (215)

By Federal Law or Policy 8.7% (39)

■ To provide an example of how these mass shooters may think, the Aurora theater shooter had at least seven movie theaters to choose from, all within a 20-minute drive of his home and all that were showing *The Dark Knight Rises*. The Century Theater that he settled on wasn't the closest (in fact, the closest was walking distance from his apartment), but it happened to be the only theater that posted "no guns" signs, while the other six theaters had no such declaration. Those "no guns" signs let the attacker know that he'd get the five to nine minutes he needed.

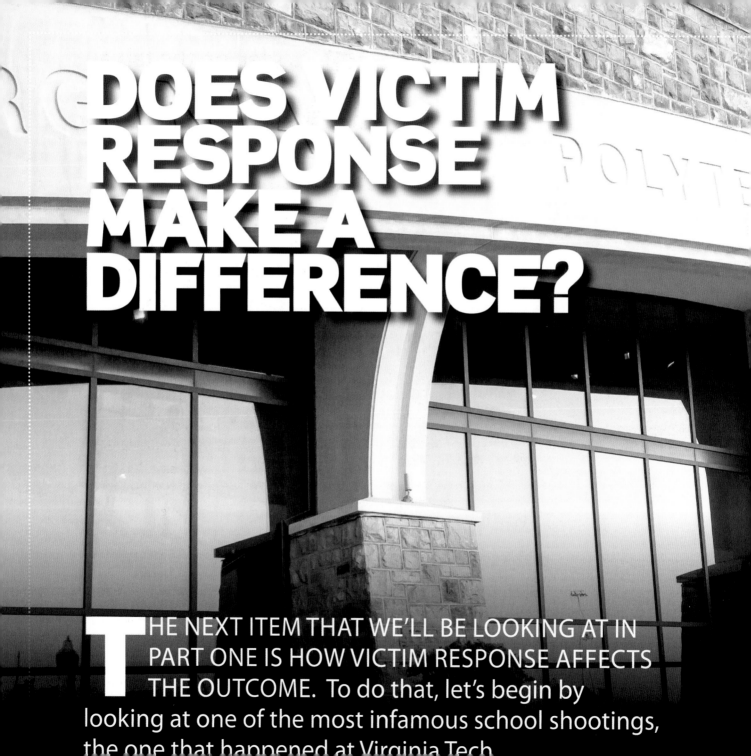

DOES VICTIM RESPONSE MAKE A DIFFERENCE?

THE NEXT ITEM THAT WE'LL BE LOOKING AT IN PART ONE IS HOW VICTIM RESPONSE AFFECTS THE OUTCOME. To do that, let's begin by looking at one of the most infamous school shootings, the one that happened at Virginia Tech.

As seen on the table shown earlier, Virginia Tech shooter was able to murder 30 students and teachers by taking advantage of 11 minutes that he had in the "gun-free zone" of Norris Hall on the Virginia Tech campus.

The assailant didn't depend on a high rate of fire. In fact, his rate of fire was half of what Union soldiers achieved with the lever-action Henry rifle. But he knew that no armed response would come from within the walls of the university building where he chose to mount his attack. He knew that an armed response would only come from outside the school walls, so a high rate of fire wasn't important to him. Skill with his two handguns was also unimportant. The gunman legally purchased both of the handguns he used during his attack, one purchased in February and the second in March, for his attack in April. No evidence exists that the shooter had taken any firearms training or had any significant practice with his firearms before the attack. So if he wasn't depending upon a high rate of fire or shooting skill, what was he depending upon?

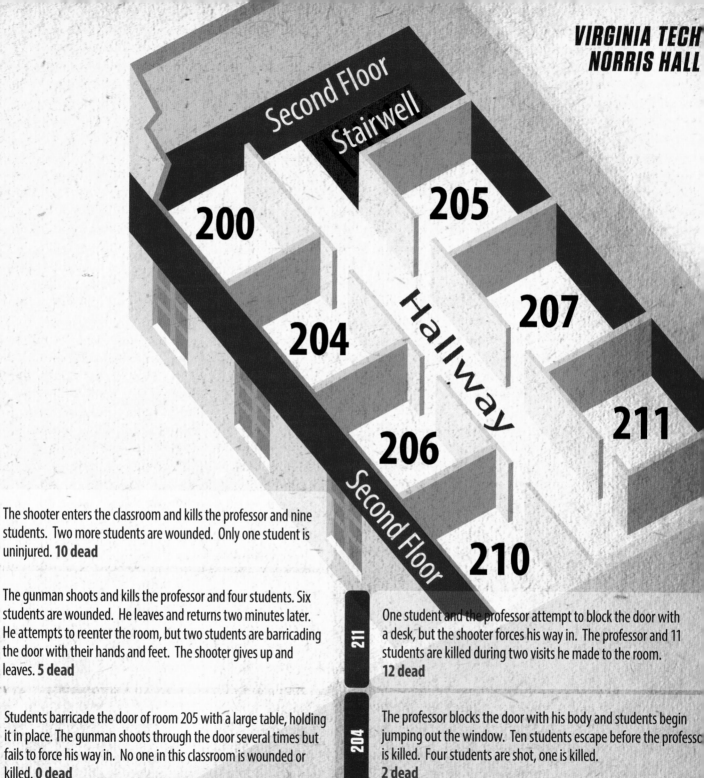

VIRGINIA TECH NORRIS HALL

Second Floor Stairwell

200

205

207

204

Hallway

211

206

Second Floor

210

206 The shooter enters the classroom and kills the professor and nine students. Two more students are wounded. Only one student is uninjured. **10 dead**

207 The gunman shoots and kills the professor and four students. Six students are wounded. He leaves and returns two minutes later. He attempts to reenter the room, but two students are barricading the door with their hands and feet. The shooter gives up and leaves. **5 dead**

205 Students barricade the door of room 205 with a large table, holding it in place. The gunman shoots through the door several times but fails to force his way in. No one in this classroom is wounded or killed. **0 dead**

211 One student and the professor attempt to block the door with a desk, but the shooter forces his way in. The professor and 11 students are killed during two visits he made to the room. **12 dead**

204 The professor blocks the door with his body and students begin jumping out the window. Ten students escape before the professor is killed. Four students are shot, one is killed. **2 dead**

After chaining the doors of Norris hall, the gunman entered or attempted to enter five separate classrooms in the sequence shown on the opposite page during his 11-minute siege. But that diagram doesn't tell the entire story. For that, you'll need to look at the diagram on the next page, which groups the classrooms by how the students and professors responded to Cho's attack.

In that diagram, Group One shows classrooms where the students and professor proactively defended the classroom from the outset by barricading the door or attempting an escape. Group Two shows classrooms where students failed to initially form a defense, but then regrouped and actively worked to barricade the classroom door. Group Three shows classrooms that could not mount or could not maintain a defense during the attack.

The second diagram clearly shows that the outcome was not consistent among the five classrooms. When students and professors actively mounted and maintained a defense, chances of survival dramatically improved, and not by just a small margin. For example, the students in classroom 205 didn't need to disable or kill the assailant. All they needed to do was delay his entry long enough for him to become frustrated and move on to a new set of targets. The shooter knew the clock was ticking, and he wasn't about to waste more than a few seconds trying to gain access to any one classroom. The result was that everyone in classroom 205 lived.

Although the students and professor in classrooms 204, 205 and 207 took (or eventually took) defensive action by barricading the classroom doors, no evidence exists showing that any student in any classroom took offensive measures, such as throwing objects at the perpetrator, striking him with objects or attempting to tackle him.

One student from room 211 was even quoted as saying that he was "waiting for it to be his turn" to be shot. Although that student heard the gunman reload three times (in fact, he reloaded 15 times total), the student failed to use the opportunities to flee the classroom or to make a counterattack. Instead, he decided to continue to wait for it to be "his turn" to die.

Please understand, I am not trying to blame the victims with this analysis. I'm simply attempting to understand what we might take away from the volumes of data that were recorded about this incident. The fact is, with no training at home or at school about what to do in the event of a mass shooting, it's unrealistic to expect the average student to come up with a plan at the moment that the gunfire erupts. That lack of training is one of four major points of failure at Virginia Tech.

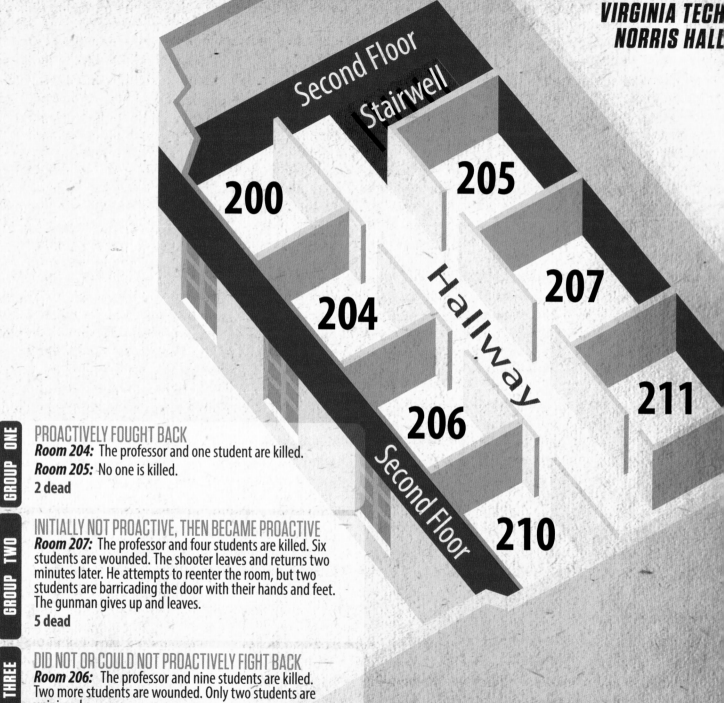

VIRGINIA TECH
NORRIS HALL

Second Floor
Stairwell

200

205

204

207

Hallway

206

211

Second Floor

210

GROUP ONE

PROACTIVELY FOUGHT BACK
Room 204: The professor and one student are killed.
Room 205: No one is killed.
2 dead

GROUP TWO

INITIALLY NOT PROACTIVE, THEN BECAME PROACTIVE
Room 207: The professor and four students are killed. Six students are wounded. The shooter leaves and returns two minutes later. He attempts to reenter the room, but two students are barricading the door with their hands and feet. The gunman gives up and leaves.
5 dead

GROUP THREE

DID NOT OR COULD NOT PROACTIVELY FIGHT BACK
Room 206: The professor and nine students are killed. Two more students are wounded. Only two students are uninjured.
Room 211: The professor and 11 students are killed.
22 dead

FOUR FAILURES

1. Doors Without Locks

The most obvious failure at Virginia Tech was the fact that the classroom doors lacked even basic locks, forcing the professors and students to block the doors with their hands and feet, which was an incredibly brave act. If the classroom doors had even a basic deadbolt, every student and professor in every classroom other than the first attacked could have been saved. If the classrooms had auto-locking doors, it's very likely that everyone would have lived. I'll add that, in my opinion, this fact was the most obvious failure in the review of the event commissioned by the Virginia governor. In that report, the panel only gave a lukewarm nod to having locks on classroom doors when they remarked, "the panel generally thought having locks on classroom doors was a good idea." As far as I know, no locks have ever been added to the classroom doors in Norris Hall.

2. No Student or Staff Training

The second major failure at Virginia Tech is the fact that no training had been provided to students regarding what actions to take if an active shooter entered the buildings. Keep in mind, this was almost eight years to the day after the Columbine shooting, so mass shootings at schools was not an unthinkable event. Had students been trained to jump into action at the first sound of gunfire, they could have effectively barricaded the doors with multiple tables and desks. Or they could have all picked up an object to hurl at the attacker if he made entry. We'll spend quite a bit more time talking about this idea in Part Two.

In the formal review, the panel made no recommendation that students and staff be provided with any training whatsoever, such as the Department of Homeland Security's, "Run, Hide, Fight" program. The panel's *only* recommendation that could fall under the subject of "training" was to make sure that students were aware that they could receive text alerts in the event that an active shooter was on campus. What the students were supposed to do *after* receiving an alert was not addressed.

3. Campus Was a Gun-Free Zone

The third failure at Virginia Tech is that the school was a self-declared gun-free zone. The gunman knew beyond a shadow of a doubt that he'd be the only armed person in Norris Hall for at least 9 to 10 minutes. We'll also spend more time talking about this data point in Part Two.

4. Missing Data on Shooter

The fourth and final major failure at Virginia Tech was the fact that even though the attacker had been adjudicated mentally ill approximately 14 months before the shooting, that information never made it from Virginia to the federal NICS database. That gap has now been filled by HR 2640, which, in part, mandates improvements in state reporting to the National Instant Criminal Background Check System in order to block gun purchases by those declared mentally ill but who are not institutionalized. Of course, had he been blocked from purchasing his firearms, it's unknown whether he would have found another source for an illegal purchase, but this was still an important gap to fill.

WHEN VICTIMS FIGHT BACK AND *WIN*

So how about potential mass shootings where the victims fought back offensively, either individually or as a team? In case after case, it can be shown that an active response by bystanders can end these shootings early, effectively saving countless lives. Let's take a look at five examples.

1 ■ THURSTON HIGH SCHOOL, SPRINGFIELD, OREGON, MAY 1998

Recently suspended Kip Kinkel entered the school with two pistols and a .22 caliber rifle. He fired a total of 50 rounds from his rifle, striking 37 people and killing two. But when he paused to reload, student Jacob Ryker (who had already been wounded) tackled him, and six other students joined in to assist. As a team, the seven students restrained Kinkel until police arrived. Although he was carrying a total of 1,127 rounds of ammunition, the proactive and aggressive counterattack by the students ended the attack after he'd fired less than 5 percent of his total ammunition.

Lessons Learned:

- *A team-based counterattack, even by unarmed defenders, can be highly successful. Ryker recognized that his only option was to fight and when other students joined in, the momentum rapidly shifted.*

2 ■ APPALACHIAN SCHOOL OF LAW, GRUNDY, VIRGINIA, JANUARY 2002

At approximately 1:00 p.m., a 43-year-old former student shot and killed Dean Anthony Sutin, Professor Thomas Blackwell and student Angela Dales, and wounded three other students. As the shooter exited the building still in possession of his handgun, he was immediately confronted by two students who had retrieved their own firearms from their vehicles; the Appalachian School of Law was a gun-free zone, and students were not allowed to carry firearms on campus. Upon seeing firearms pointed at him by both Tracy Bridges and Mikael Gross, the gunman dropped his firearm and was subdued.

Lessons Learned:

- *By declaring the campus a gun-free zone, the administration created the perfect environment for a mentally deranged individual to commit this crime. Had Bridges and Gross not been able to quickly access their firearms from their vehicles, the shooter would almost certainly have continued his rampage.*

3 ■ NEW LIFE CHURCH, COLORADO SPRINGS, COLORADO, DECEMBER 2007

Thirty minutes after the morning service had ended, the shooter exited his vehicle and opened fire on three vehicles as they were leaving the parking lot, killing two and wounding two, before heading toward the main entrance of the church where hundreds of people were still gathered in the main hallway. Inside the church, Jeanne Assam, who was a member of New Life's formal armed volunteer program, began to move toward the sound of gunfire. After seeing the shooter enter the main doors, Assam

took cover in a side hallway and listened as the gunman began to advance, firing at parishioners who had not yet escaped. Assam then stepped out from behind cover and shouted for him to drop his weapon. The assailant refused and turned his rifle toward Assam, who fired five rounds, with at least two rounds striking the shooter. Although Assam believes she fired the fatal shot, the subsequent coroner's report indicated that the gunman killed himself with a pistol. Police reports showed that the attacker had in his possession more than 1,000 rounds of ammunition and that approximately 7,000 people were on the church campus at the time of the shooting.

Lessons Learned:
- *New Life Church had developed*

an Emergency Operations Plan in advance, which included an armed volunteer program. Had Assam and other armed volunteers not been on the scene, it's likely that dozens more would have been killed before police arrived, which was approximately five minutes after the shooting had ended.
- *Although Assam gave the shooter a verbal warning before returning fire, it's worth noting that only four percent of active shooters surrender. We'll talk about the legal and ethical rules governing the use of deadly force during mass shootings in Part Two, including whether a verbal warning is required or even advised.*

4 ■ LA TOSCANA VILLAGE MALL, TUCSON, ARIZONA, JANUARY 2011

Jared Loughner fired 31 rounds into a crowd attending a constituent

Nestled in the lowlands below the Garden of the Gods, New Life Church is home to more than 10,000 members. The main sanctuary can seat more than 5,000 and the theater seats another 1,500. On December 9, 2007 there were more than 7,000 members and visitors on campus when a gunman opened fire, killing two and wounding three. He had in his possession more than 1,000 rounds of ammunition when he was shot by armed volunteer Jeanne Assam.

meeting hosted by Rep. Gabriel Giffords. When attempting to reload, he dropped the magazine. While one bystander fought the shooter for the dropped magazine, three other bystanders tackled him to the ground, including 74-year-old retired Army Col. Bill Badger (who was wounded), as well as Joseph Zamudio and Roger Sulzgeber. Although six innocent people lost their lives during this shooting, far more would have been injured or killed if it weren't for the proactive and aggressive actions of his potential victims.

Lessons Learned:

- *Since most mass shooters fire at their victims from contact distances, that close proximity can work in favor of victims mounting a counterattack. Although the attacker's rate of fire was the highest recorded by any mass shooter at two rounds per second, that rate was still too slow to shoot everyone who was counterattacking him simultaneously.*
- *Even when it is uncoordinated, a team-based counterattack can be extremely effective.*

5 ■ THALYS HIGH-SPEED TRAIN, EN ROUTE BETWEEN BELGIUM AND PARIS, AUGUST 2015

At approximately 5:45 p.m. local time, 25-year-old assailant exited a restroom armed with an AK-47 and a Luger pistol. The gunman was carrying nine additional magazines for his AK-47 for a total of 270 rounds. Immediately upon exiting the restroom, a French passenger identified only as Damien A. confronted the gunman and attempted to wrestle the AK-47 away from him. After breaking free, the shooter entered the next train compartment where 51-year-old American-born Mark Moogalain also attempted to disarm him. While attempting to shoot Moogalain, the rifle malfunctioned. Unable to fire the rifle, the shooter drew his pistol. During the ensuing struggle, the magazine release was pressed on the Luger, dropping the magazine to the floor. Moogalain was subsequently shot in the neck with the single round remaining in the gun. Upon hearing the gunshot and struggle, three Americans, including university student Anthony Sadler, U.S. Airman First Class Spencer Stone and Oregon National Guard Specialist Alek Skarlatos, joined the counterattack. Stone immediately charged the gunman, slamming into him and knocking the rifle out of his hands. Skarlatos then disarmed the attacker of the pistol and attempted to shoot him with it, before realizing that the pistol was already empty. The three Americans then surrounded the shooter (now armed only with a box cutter) and began punching him simultaneously. Stone placed the gunman into a chokehold rendering him unconscious, but not before Stone's thumb was nearly severed with the box cutter. The heroics didn't end there. After subduing the shooter, Stone, a trained medic, recognized that the gunshot injury to Moogalain's neck had lacerated an artery, which was bleeding profusely. Stone inserted his fingers directly into the gunshot wound, found the bleeding artery and pinched it off, ultimately saving Moogalain's life. With more than 500 passengers onboard the speeding train and no armed security, this attack had the potential of eclipsing the attack on the Bataclan theatre in Paris in November 2015, which killed 89 people.

Lessons Learned:

- *The more quickly a counterattack can be launched, the more quickly the shooter's momentum can be broken. When Damien A. and Mark Moogalain attacked the shooter before he had a chance to fire his first round, the result was a single-shot pistol and a disabled rifle. The initial counterattack also gave the three additional defenders time to join in, ultimately subduing the attacker before anyone was killed.*

- *Attacking as a team was critical in this situation. The assailant was able to get past the first defender and wound the second defender. If just a single counterattacker had joined in the fight at that point, it's possible that the shooter could have cleared his AK-47's malfunction or retrieved the magazine for his pistol and continued his attack. The three Americans simultaneously attacking the assailant from all sides made the difference.*

- *Since mass shooters may be armed with multiple weapons, counterattackers should not give up until the shooter is completely disabled, unconscious or dead.*

- *Immediate first aid rendered to injured victims is critical. Mark Moogalain almost certainly would have died had it not been for the live-saving treatment provided by Airman Stone.*

■For their part in repelling the Paris train attack, Americans Anthony Sadler, Airman Spencer Stone and Specialist Alek Skarlatos, along with French-American Mark Moogalain, were awarded the Chevaliers de la Légion d'honneur by French President Francois Hollande. The three Americans were also honored in the U.S. with Sadler receiving the Secretary of Defense Medal for Valor; Skarlatos receiving the Soldier's Medal (the highest award for actions not taken in combat); and Stone receiving the Airman's Medal and the Purple Heart.

WHAT ARE UNIVERSAL BACKGROUND CHECKS AND WOULD THEY END MASS SHOOTINGS?

A "UNIVERSAL BACKGROUND CHECK" LAW would require all sales of all firearms between private individuals to be transacted through federally licensed firearms dealers, at which time a Form 4473 background check occur. But would universal background checks have prevented any of the 48 mass shootings that have occurred since Columbine?

Current law in the U.S. requires that when a firearm is purchased through a federally licensed dealer (FFL), the buyer is required to fill out ATF form 4473 and subsequently pass a NICS background check before they take possession of the firearm.

But in many U.S. states, sales of firearms between individuals are not subject to the same background checks required at FFLs. That means that a neighbor can sell a firearm to a neighbor or a father can sell a gun to his daughter without bringing the feds into the matter. That doesn't, of course, mean that the seller is off the hook; all states have a provision in their law that states if a seller transfers a firearm to an individual that the seller knows is ineligible, or if the seller knows or *should* know that the buyer will commit a crime with the firearm, the seller is getting charged with a felony. That provision is enough that most private sellers will either sell to an individual known to them, or they will ask to see a concealed carry permit or a permit to purchase a firearm document before making the sale, which would indicate that the buyer has passed a background check. But what about if a buyer purchases a gun off the internet — does that gun get shipped directly to the buyer's house, skipping the background check? The answer is absolutely not. This is one of the greatest fallacies of anti-gun lore. Any time a firearm is shipped, it *must* be shipped to an FFL, and the FFL will *only* release the gun after the buyer has passed a background check. There are a number of popular firearm auction and online websites, and each mandates (and the sellers must obey) the requirement that all firearms shipments follow this federal regulation. If you hear a news commentator discuss how "internet sales" allow buyers to skip the background check, they

■ *While there are a number of popular firearms auction sites such as GunBroker.com, these sites do not ship directly between buyer and seller. Instead, they require that any firearm purchased be shipped to an FFL, and the FFL will conduct a background check prior to releasing it to the buyer. If the buyer fails the background check, the firearm is shipped back to the seller.*

■ What exactly is the "gun show loophole?" The "gun show loophole" refers to the fact that in many states in the U.S., sales of firearms between individuals are not subject to the same background checks that are required at federally licensed firearms dealers (FFLs). That means that a neighbor can sell a firearm to a neighbor or a father can sell a gun to his daughter, without bringing the feds into the sale. The reason this has been referred to as the "gun show loophole" in the past is that at some gun shows, private transactions are allowed between individuals who are not affiliated with an FFL. In other words, if a buyer purchased a gun from the Smith & Wesson booth, they would be required to pass a background check. But if two visitors decided to conduct a transaction between themselves, it would be considered a private sale in many states, and no background check would be required. This phrase has recently lost favor, and gun control advocates now refer to this as a proposal to enact "universal background checks" rather than the need to close a "loophole."

69

clearly have no idea what they're talking about. As an example, after the San Bernardino shooting, one interviewee on CNN referred to how gun buyers could purchase guns from Craigslist and then meet the seller in person, thereby completing the sale without conducting a background check. The problem with that statement is that it's a lie. Craigslist doesn't allow firearms sales on its website anywhere in the country. So much for honest dialogue about this topic.

So universal background checks would change nothing when it comes to firearms purchased through dealers or websites, which, as explained, already require that firearms be shipped to an FFL before being picked up by the buyer. So universal background checks would only affect private sales between individuals conducting legal firearms transfers in person.

So that begs the question: how many of the 48 mass shootings that have occurred since 1998 (which is the year that background checks began) would have been blocked if universal background checks had been required?

FIREARM TRANSFERS

Since NICS checks became the law in November of 1998, transfers of firearms could be lumped into four categories:

1. Firearms purchased from federally licensed dealers (FFLs), which accounts for the vast majority of gun transfers in the U.S. These sales require that the buyer fill out ATF form 4473 and subsequently pass a NICS background check. This category would also include any firearm purchased on an internet site, which as mentioned, must be shipped to an FFL rather than having it shipped directly to the buyer's home.

2. Firearms that are "transferred" through theft.

3. Transfers which the buyer and seller know are illegal sales (which is different than the next category of legal, private sales).

4. The final category is legal transfers between private parties that don't require a background check in many states. This is the *only* category of transfer being targeted by proposed universal background checks.

■ ATF form 4473 must be filled out any time a firearm is purchased from an FFL or when a firearm is purchased over the internet, which must be shipped to an FFL for transfer to the buyer. The FFL will then run a background check through the federal government's NICS system before completing or denying the transfer.

So for us to know how many of the 48 mass shootings since 1998 would have been blocked if universal background checks were required, it's necessary to look at the source of every one of the firearms used in those 48 cases. That data has been summarized on the charts on the next few pages.

1. Guns Purchased with a Background Check

The chart below highlights the events where the shooter legally purchased their firearm or firearms from a federally licensed dealer after successfully passing a background check. In other words, in 38 of the 48 events since Columbine, the shooter was able to walk into a federally licensed dealer, fill out form 4473, pass a background check and walk out with the firearm or firearms. Keep in mind that those who are calling for universal background checks aren't proposing that the background check be made more difficult to pass; they simply want more people to take the check. So universal background checks would have done nothing to prevent these 38 shootings.

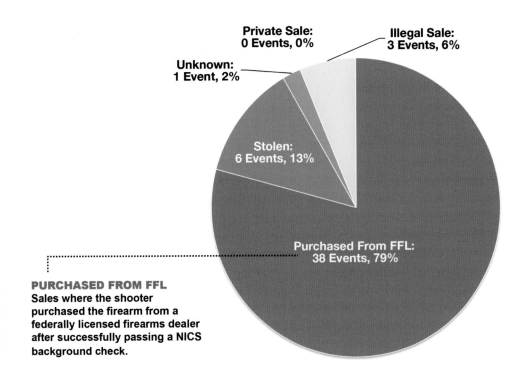

Private Sale:
0 Events, 0%

Illegal Sale:
3 Events, 6%

Unknown:
1 Event, 2%

Stolen:
6 Events, 13%

Purchased From FFL:
38 Events, 79%

PURCHASED FROM FFL
Sales where the shooter purchased the firearm from a federally licensed firearms dealer after successfully passing a NICS background check.

2. Stolen Guns

In six of the events, the firearm or firearms used were stolen from another party. As shown on the chart below, in four of the events, the gun was stolen from a family member, and in two cases, the gun was stolen during a robbery and subsequently used in the mass shooting. Since thieves don't fill out paperwork, universal background checks would have had no affect on these six mass shootings.

3. Illegal Sales

Let's take a deeper dive into what an *illegal* sale might be, which occurred in three of the 48 mass shootings. Typically, an illegal sale is a sale in which the seller or

sellers know in advance that the sale is illegal, either because the buyer is underage or because the buyer has disqualifying crimes on his or her record.

In one event, a buyer purchased two guns from an FFL on behalf of another individual who wanted to avoid having the firearms linked to his name. This constituted an illegal "straw" sale, even though the ultimate buyer was not ineligible to purchase a gun and would have passed a background check himself. That event was the San Bernardino shooting. At the time of the attack, the individual who obtained the guns was a U.S. citizen and had no disqualifying crimes on his background that would have prevented him from purchasing the two AR-15s used. In other words, he could have walked into

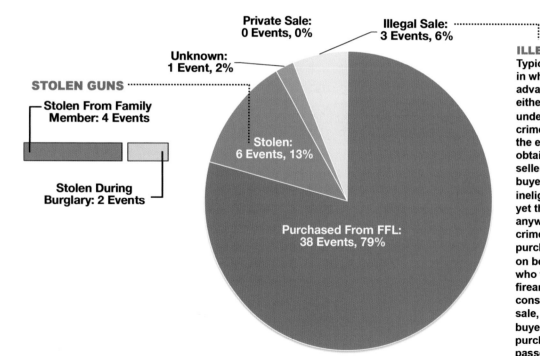

STOLEN GUNS
- Stolen From Family Member: 4 Events
- Stolen During Burglary: 2 Events

Private Sale: 0 Events, 0%
Unknown: 1 Event, 2%
Illegal Sale: 3 Events, 6%
Stolen: 6 Events, 13%
Purchased From FFL: 38 Events, 79%

ILLEGAL SALES
Typically, an illegal sale is a sale in which the seller(s) know in advance that the sale is illegal, either because the buyer is underage, or has disqualifying crimes on their record. In two of the events where the guns were obtained through illegal sales, the sellers knew in advance that the buyers were underage and were ineligible to purchase a firearm, yet they completed the sale anyway, knowingly committing a crime. In the third, a buyer purchased two guns from an FFL on behalf of another individual who wanted to avoid having the firearms linked to his name. This constituted an illegal "straw" sale, even though the ultimate buyer was not ineligible to purchase a gun, and would have passed a background check himself.

■The San Bernardino assailant was a U.S. citizen and had no disqualifying crimes on his background that would have prevented him from purchasing the two AR-15s used in the attack. In other words, he could have walked into a federally licensed dealer, passed a background check and legally purchased the guns. In fact, that's exactly what he did when he purchased the two handguns used in the attack.

Photo by Sean M. Haffey/Getty Images

a federally licensed dealer, passed a background check and legally purchased the guns. In fact, that's exactly what he did when he purchased the two handguns used in the attack. But instead of purchasing the AR-15s on his own, the shooter asked his friend to make the purchase on his behalf. Regardless of whether Marquez was part of the terrorist plot, he was guilty of conducting an illegal straw purchase, though an unusual straw purchase. Typically, a straw purchase occurs when the ultimate buyer is ineligible to purchase a gun, which in this case wasn't true since the attacker-to-be had already passed a required background check once and would have passed again in purchasing the AR-15s from an FFL himself. The prevailing theory at the time I compiled this data is that the shooter went to his friend because he wanted to avoid having his name associated with so many firearms purchases, which he believed could have given away his terrorist plot. But we know that in this case, no such red flag would have been raised, and he would have passed the background check had he purchased the AR-15s on his own. In other words, universal background checks would have made no difference in this case.

In two other events where the guns were obtained through illegal sales, the sellers knew in advance that the buyers were underage and were ineligible to purchase firearms. They completed the sale anyway, knowingly committing a crime. One of those events was the Columbine shooting. So couldn't the Columbine shooting have been avoided if universal background checks had been required, since those guns sales were between private parties?

The answer is no. As underage buyers, the Columbine shooters knew that the only way to purchase firearms would be through an illegal sale, and they found two willing sellers. Since they were too young to purchase firearms on their own, they paid a friend to purchase three firearms on their behalf. When the friend complied, she was guilty of conducting an illegal straw purchase. A fourth firearm was purchased from another seller who also knew that the boys were underage but sold to them anyway. It's incredibly unlikely that an additional law would have given either the buyers or the sellers pause in this case, as criminals are notoriously unconcerned with following the law.

As underage buyers, the Columbine shooters knew that the only way to purchase firearms would be through an illegal sale, and they found two willing sellers.

4. Private Sales

Now let's zero in on private sales, which are sales between individuals where no background check is required and, of course, the type of sales that Barack Obama, Hillary Clinton and other gun-control advocates would like to eliminate, each using mass shootings as the justification for taking this measure. The problem is not one mass shooting involved a gun that was acquired through a legal private sale. Not a single one.

So let's ask this question again: How many of the 48 mass shootings since 1998 would have been blocked if universal background checks were required? The answer is none. Like a reduction in magazine capacity, universal background checks are "feel-good" solutions that would have had absolutely no effect on the 48 mass shootings that have occurred since Columbine, and there is no evidence that they would reduce the current trajectory of mass shootings in the U.S. This is another one of those solutions that are referred to as, "common-sense solutions" by gun-control advocates.

But isn't it common sense to propose something that would actually make a difference?

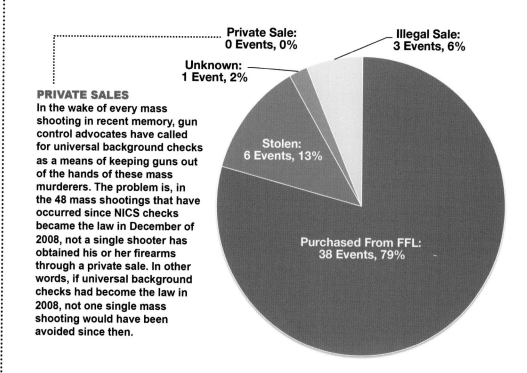

PRIVATE SALES
In the wake of every mass shooting in recent memory, gun control advocates have called for universal background checks as a means of keeping guns out of the hands of these mass murderers. The problem is, in the 48 mass shootings that have occurred since NICS checks became the law in December of 2008, not a single shooter has obtained his or her firearms through a private sale. In other words, if universal background checks had become the law in 2008, not one single mass shooting would have been avoided since then.

Private Sale:
0 Events, 0%

Illegal Sale:
3 Events, 6%

Unknown:
1 Event, 2%

Stolen:
6 Events, 13%

Purchased From FFL:
38 Events, 79%

WHAT ABOUT NO-FLY LISTS AND TERRORIST WATCH LISTS?

AT THE FIRST PRESIDENTIAL DEBATE BETWEEN HILLARY CLINTON AND DONALD TRUMP, Clinton proposed that the U.S., "Pass a prohibition from purchasing a firearm for anyone on the terrorist watch list." But how many innocent people end up getting added to the list, and would that prohibition have prevented any mass shooting in the past or have any hope of preventing mass shootings in the future?

Now this proposal sounds like it has some merit. After all, if the U.S. government doesn't trust someone to fly, or if an agency of the government has added the person's name to a terrorist watch list, why would we trust that person to purchase a firearm?

Before we attempt to answer that question, let's first talk about the lists themselves. In the first presidential debate and in the debate in congress after the shooting in Orlando, Florida, two lists were thrown about including the "Terror Watch List" (more properly called the Terrorist Screening Database, or TSDB) and the "no-fly" list. These aren't actually two separate lists — the no-fly list is a smaller subset of the much larger TSDB. Just how large are the lists? In June of 2016, the FBI and National Counterterrorism Center (NCTC) jointly responding to a congressional inquiry, indicated that the TSDB contained approximately one million names, while the no-fly list contained approximately 81,000. While most of the discussion around using these lists as disqualifiers for firearms purchases has centered around the no-fly list, Clinton referred to the much larger list during the presidential debate. So back to the question posed earlier: if the U.S. government doesn't trust someone to fly or if they've included a name on the terrorist watch list, doesn't it make sense to bar that person from purchasing a firearm?

Well, there are really two problems with that thinking.

First, there is simply no due process for when a name is added to either list. In a 166-page guideline issued by the National Counterterrorism Center titled, *March 2013 Watchlisting Guidance*, the government's secret rules for placing individuals on the TSDB and the no-fly list was spelled out.

The document revealed that the rules required

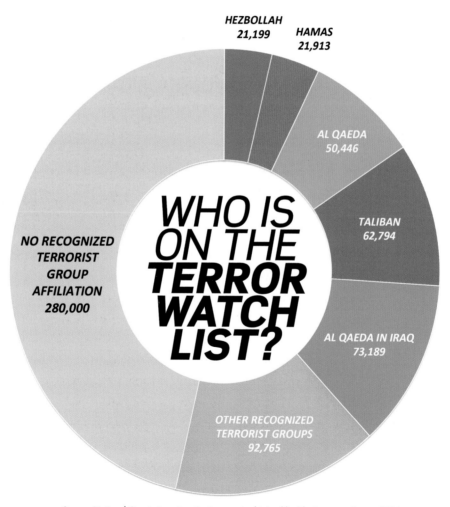

HEZBOLLAH
21,199

HAMAS
21,913

AL QAEDA
50,446

TALIBAN
62,794

AL QAEDA IN IRAQ
73,189

OTHER RECOGNIZED TERRORIST GROUPS
92,765

NO RECOGNIZED TERRORIST GROUP AFFILIATION
280,000

WHO IS ON THE TERROR WATCH LIST?

Source: National Counterterrorism Center report, obtained by *The Intercept*, August 2014

2001

16 People
On the "No Transport" List

2016

81,000 People
On the "No-Fly" List

Source: National Counterterrorism Center (NCTC) and the Federal Bureau of Investigation.

neither "concrete facts" nor "irrefutable evidence" to designate an American or a foreigner as a terrorist; and instead, the guidelines say agencies can "nominate" individuals for the list if there is a "reasonable suspicion" to believe they are a "known or suspected terrorist." That's a pretty low bar by anyone's measure.

While we'd love to trust our government, America's democracy is really built on questioning our government, and unfortunately, the U.S. government has a checkered history of building secret lists of people who'd broken no laws but who secret committees deemed dangerous to American interests. FBI director J. Edgar Hoover had such a list that he titled, "Enemies of the United States." Some notable names were on it, including Dr. Martin Luther King, Jr.

Think about it this way: While gun purchases are a hot-button issue, the public's thinking on these lists might change if the government suggested that people on the lists should be banned from purchasing homes, "in order to deny possible terrorists a base of operations." Or that warrantless wiretaps should be allowed for anyone on the lists. Or that people on the list be barred from voting, "in order to deny terrorists an ability to influence American elections." What would you do if *your* name was on those secret lists?

If either list is to be used as an additional disqualifier

for purchasing a firearm, they simply *must* have better oversight than a secretive government body making the decision about who goes on the lists, and the procedures for having your name removed from the list must be clearly stated. If you believe that these lists are only made up of foreign-based fighters just itching to take down

the San Bernardino mass shooters, who were Muslim extremists. Yet, four days after the San Bernardino shooting, President Obama proposed this as one of the solutions in preventing future mass shootings. Why would he have proposed a solution that wouldn't have prevented the shooting that just occurred?

■ *While we'd love to trust our government, America's democracy is really built on questioning our government, and unfortunately, the U.S. government has a checkered history of building secret lists of people who'd broken no laws but who secret committees deemed as dangerous to America. FBI director J. Edgar Hoover had such a list that he titled, "Enemies of the United States." Some notable names were on it, including Dr. Martin Luther King, Jr.*

the U.S., think again. Many prominent Americans have been caught up in the lists including antiwar activists Jan Adams and Rebecca Gordan, Sen. Ted Kennedy, civil rights attorney David Cole, and even singer Cat Stevens.

Now let's bring the topic back to how this proposal might have an effect on mass shootings. The fact is, not a single mass shooter in U.S. history has ever been on the TSDB or the no-fly list. Not one, and that's including

We all want simple solutions to this problem, but this proposal is yet another one of those "feel-good" measures that would have had no effect on past mass shootings, and there is no evidence to indicate that it would have an effect on future mass shootings.

On the surface, barring individuals who are on the terrorist watch list or the "no-fly" list from purchasing firearms sounds like it has some merit. But the problem is, there's no due process for how a name is added to or removed from the list. The greater problem is that no mass shooter in U.S. history has even been on either list. That includes the ISIS-inspired mass shooters who struck in San Bernardino and at the Pulse nightclub in Orlando, Florida. Using the lists as an additional disqualifier for firearm purchases would not have prevented those attacks, or any of the other mass shootings that have occurred since or before Columbine.

PART ONE SUMMARY

IN THE INTRODUCTION, I EXPLAINED THAT MY GOAL WITH ALL OF THE RESEARCH THAT I'D DONE WAS TO ANSWER THE QUESTION: WHAT CAN COUNTER THIS THREAT? I was willing to follow the data and the evidence wherever it took me. If the data told me that one or more of the solutions proposed by gun control advocates would work, then I was prepared to embrace those solutions. But if not, I was ready to propose something new.

I will summarize the evidence gathered for Part One with this observation: Since Columbine, the U.S. has experienced 48 mass shootings. The solutions proposed by Barack Obama, Hillary Clinton and other gun-control advocates have included limitations on magazine capacity, banning AR-15s, universal background checks and, most recently, barring individuals from purchasing firearms who are on the federal terrorist watch list or the "no-fly" list.

The evidence clearly shows that if these proposals had all been passed, en masse, just before Columbine, they would not have prevented even one of the 48 mass shootings. Not one. Nor would those proposals have saved a single life during any mass shooting. Needless to say, I'm ready to propose something new. But first, let's review what we've learned.

It's Not the Magazines, It's the Time

The volume of data we reviewed in Part One clearly indicates that the large number of victims murdered during mass shootings is not occurring because of magazine capacity or because the murderers have chosen one firearm type over another or one caliber over another. Instead, the number of deaths can be directly attributed to the uninterrupted time that these attackers have alone with their victims in a gun-free zone. Even

It's the Time

Even excluding Columbine and Orlando (events which lasted dramatically longer than the average event), the average duration for the 20 worst mass shootings in the U.S. is nine minutes.

excluding Columbine and the Pulse nightclub in Orlando from the calculation, the average duration for the 20 worst mass shootings in the U.S. since Columbine is nine minutes. Nine long minutes where the only person on the scene with a gun is the attacker While that may not sound like a lot of time, it's enough time to

murder 108 unarmed people using nothing more than a single-shot Sharps rifle and a bag full of ammunition. When no one is shooting back, nine minutes is all the time in the world. That needs to change.

Gun-Free Zones Are Killing Zones

With 85 percent of the deaths from mass shootings occurring in areas where private citizens were either disarmed by state law, school policy, federal law or policy, or by private policy, it is no longer possible to pretend that "gun-free zones" are not synonymous with "killing zones." No history of a mass shooter fighting his way through hardened physical security or past armed defenders exists, and for a very simple reason. Mass shooters want to be known for one thing only: body count. Given the choice, the potential mass shooter will pick a soft target every single time.

Fighting Back Makes a Difference

The data also proves that an active response by potential victims affects the outcome. That active response might be barricading a door, running away, escaping from a window or fighting back. In all cases, survival jumps exponentially. Fighting back as a team *significantly* affects the shooter's ability to continue his attack. But as witnessed at Virginia Tech, without formal training at school, at work, at your house of worship or at home, we cannot expect the average person to come up with a plan at the moment that the gunfire erupts. But it does happen. Earlier in Part One, we saw data which showed that in nearly one out of five active shooting events tracked by the FBI, the shooter was subdued or shot by his potential victims. Formalizing a program that teaches students, parishioners, employees and everyone else to run, hide or fight will not only increase the number of events being stopped by potential victims, it will shorten the duration of these events and save lives.

A 9/11 Level Response Is Needed

In the introduction, I shared the unease that I felt when my youngest son asked me whether I thought a bad man with a gun might ever attack his school. I feel a bit more confident in my answers when I assure my son that terrorists will never again take over airplanes and fly them into buildings. But for that answer, I have a bit more to fall back on considering the response that the nation took after 9/11 compared to its response after the attack on Sandy Hook elementary in Newtown, Connecticut. After the single lesson of 9/11, the nation went on a war footing and changed the way we protect our airports and airplanes by installing sophisticated body scanners at airports, hardening cockpit doors, creating an armed pilot program and expanding the armed air marshal program. The terrorists of 9/11

were fairly confident that if they couldn't bluff their way into the cockpit, they'd be able to breach the door, where they'd find a defenseless crew tucked into its very own gun-free zone. Today, Al-Qaeda and ISIS know that even if a cockpit door could be breached (however unlikely), there is a high probability that the terrorist's last memory would be a muzzle flash as an armed pilot shot him in the face.

But after Newtown, Virginia Tech, San Bernardino, Orlando and 44 other hard and bloody lessons, nothing has really changed for us. While the country's anti-gun forces continue to point fingers and chase red herrings, most of our nation's schools remain as unprotected as they were the day before the Newtown massacre, just as our houses of worship are as unprotected today as they were the day before the Charleston attack. Far too many of our public and private establishments remain inviting targets to mass shooters, even advertising that fact with "gun-free zone" signs, letting those potential murderers know that no one can stop them. We remain a nation where even members of the most virulent anti-gun groups have grown to not only accept, but *expect* armed guards to protect our banks, our museums, our airports, our politicians and our celebrities, yet they somehow find the thought of armed guards protecting our schools, our children and our churches abhorrent. Our priorities have been misplaced for far too long, and it's time to propose something new. That's where Part Two comes in.

→ PART TWO

COUNTERING THE THREAT

KNOW THE SIGNS

THERE IS NO SINGLE PROFILE THAT DEFINES THE MASS SHOOTER. Some could be categorized as psychotic, such as the Virginia Tech Shooter. Others, including the San Bernardino and Orlando shooters, are motivated

While no common profile exists, common indicators do ... if you know the signs. Additionally, most shooters have left a trail of physical or electronic evidence that was missed by friends or family. In 80 percent of the mass shootings since Columbine, the shooter told someone in advance about the plans, yet they weren't taken seriously.

Picking the potential mass shooter out of a crowded field of students, employees or parishioners won't be as simple as looking at what the individual is wearing or what music they are listening to. Dr. Peter Langman would agree. In his article "School Shooters: The Warning Signs", he notes, "The warning signs of school shootings do not relate to students' clothing, the video games they play, their musical preferences or other aspects of their lifestyles." In many cases however, Langman says these shooters are "very

> *These shooters are "very disempowered, not succeeding in life in multiple domains, and we see that with college and adult shooters. They're typically failing in academics, failing in the world of work, failing in the world of friendship, in romance or sexuality. Nothing really is going right in any major domain for them."*
> *Dr. Peter Langman*

disempowered, not succeeding in life in multiple domains, and we see that with college and adult shooters. They're typically failing in academics, failing in the world of work, failing in the world of friendship, in romance or sexuality. Nothing really is going right in any major domain for them."

While an outsider may believe that they are doing "okay," the potential shooter may believe that they are failing at everything, or worse, that everyone is failing them. But not all young men (or women) who are suffering one or more failures become mass shooters. So what are the warning signs that an individual may be at risk, or may have already reached the planning stage? Warning signs can be found in three different areas: Risk factors, direct indicators and indirect indicators.

Risk Factors

While the vast majority of individuals who come from broken homes or who have disengaged parents will never become mass shooters, when multiple risk factors exist, the individual should appropriately be considered at risk for violence or suicide. Risk factors can include:

- Multiple failures academically, socially or romantically.
- Troubled, broken or abusive home.
- Disengaged parents, no responsible adult providing oversight in their lives.
- Psychotic symptoms including hallucinations and delusions.

Direct Indicators

Risk factors simply indicate that an individual may be at risk, but direct indicators show that actual planning may have begun. In case after case, mass shooters have left direct indicators of their plans, either in physical or electronic form, or in what they said or did. But in far too many cases, friends or family members didn't take the indicators seriously. Direct indicators can include physical evidence, such as:

- The individual actively seeking out a friend or family member for an illegal firearm purchase when the potential shooter is underage. Not only is this a direct indicator, it's also illegal and must be reported.
- An unexplained and uncharacteristic stockpiling of firearms, ammunition or components that could be used to manufacturer an explosive.
- Written documentation such as specific plans for an attack or violent "fictional" stories written with real-world settings or actors.

- Direct warnings for friends or family members to stay away from an area on a specific date.
- Direct threats, specifically stating their grievances and/or plans verbally or in writing such as in a journal or as part of a writing assignment.

Direct Indicators on Social Media

Direct indicators can also include information left on social media such as:

- Posts expressing an admiration for past mass shooters; an admiration for ISIS, Al Quaeda or other terrorist organizations; positive references to Hitler or Nazi Germany; or comments which could be taken as thoughts of suicide.
- Photos showing the individual pointing a firearm directly at the camera or at his or her own head. If such a manual existed, both of these photos would be straight out of the "Mass Shooter's Instruction Manual."

■ The two photos of the Virginia Tech shooter pointing his guns at the camera and at his own head have been repeated countless times by other mass shooters. If you see a similar photo posted on a friend's or family member's social media site, it should be taken seriously, and reported to a trusted adult.

The steps to a "say something" campaign are simple:
1. Look for warning signs, signals and threats.
2. Act immediately, take it seriously.
3. Say something to a trusted adult.

While the direct indicators listed might seem laughably obvious, in every one of the 48 mass shootings since Columbine, those direct indicators existed and were either missed or ignored by family and friends of the shooter.

Indirect Indicators

While most mass shooters wouldn't be categorized as loners, many will be disengaged from normal social and family relationships, or they may express antisocial behavior. Other indirect indicators include:

- Socially dysfunctional.
- Difficultly relating emotionally with others.
- May show bullying tendencies. Contrary to popular belief, most mass shooters have not been bullied and instead tend to be the bully.
- Other indirect indicators can appear on social media or in writing, which may not show a specific desire for violence but can indicate feelings of despair, disenfranchisement or feeling that the world is conspiring against him or her.

To monitor students with risk factors, direct indicators or indirect indicators, Dr. Langman suggests that every student in every school have at least one direct connection with a teacher or coach. That doesn't mean that the adult simply asks the student, "How are you doing?" during the occasional hallway conversation. Instead, it means that the adult take an *actual* interest in helping the student to remain engaged, and it means taking the responsibility to monitor that student's social media usage. While other students or friends of the potential mass shooter might miss the signs or not take them seriously, having at least one responsible adult who takes a true interest in the student and his or her social media can not only help identify potential violence before it starts, it can also reduce or eliminate the possibility that violence or suicide is contemplated in the first place.

Reversing the Trend

While society as a whole is shifting to elevate fame over sacrifice, service and hard work, parents have an opportunity to counteract that pull, with the following advice:

- If your child is lacking success academically, set aside time for homework every single evening and check his or her work. Success gives rise to success, which may reveal that hard work academically can also bring success and fame.
- If your son is lacking success socially or on the playing field, encourage him to sign up for Cub Scouts, Boy Scouts or a similar organization such as your local Police or Fire Explorer post. Keep this one in mind — Eagle Scouts are not out shooting up schools, malls or churches.
- Monitor your child's social media accounts. Act like the grownup in your relationship with simple rules. If you're not allowed to monitor the social media accounts, then the social media accounts go away.
- Monitor your child's computer use. While it's possible to hide or delete web searches or create hidden files or folders, investigations post-shooting have almost always found an obvious electronic trail. Monitoring your child's computer use doesn't mean that you'll find a document labeled, "My Mass Shooting To-Do List," but it will alert you if your child is spending time on neo-Nazi forums, forums dedicated to the glorification of past mass murders or forums which advocate racist, xenophobic or homophobic views.
- It's your house. No place should be off limits to a search, whether it's searching your child's bedroom, bank statement, phone, computer, and every nook and cranny where something could be hidden.
- Be a model for your children in your behavior and actions. See the best in people, not the worst. If your dinner conversation consists of bitching about what's wrong with the world and who's to blame, you'll pass that losing attitude on to your child. While you may not turn them into a mass shooter, you will create an adult with built-in excuses on why their life is failing, rather than giving them the tools and attitude to achieve real success.

CREATE AN EMERGENCY OPERATIONS PLAN

ON MARCH 30, 2011, PRESIDENT BARACK OBAMA SIGNED PRESIDENTIAL POLICY DIRECTIVE 8, which was designed to overhaul the nation's emergency preparedness, and with it, our ability to respond to threats large and small.

The directive's stated goal was "Strengthening the security and resilience of the United States through systematic preparation for the threats that pose the greatest risk to the security of the nation, including acts of terrorism, cyber attacks, pandemics and catastrophic natural disasters."

The directive went on to say, "Our national preparedness is the shared responsibility of all levels of government, the private and nonprofit sectors, and individual citizens. Everyone can contribute to safeguarding the nation from harm. As such, while this directive is intended to galvanize action by the federal government, it is also aimed at facilitating an integrated, all-of-nation, capabilities-based approach to preparedness."

In response to this presidential directive, FEMA released a number of guidelines designed to assist houses of worship, schools and businesses in developing customized Emergency Operations Plans (EOPs) to fit the specific needs and characteristics of each institution. While I believe FEMA's step-by-step instructions and templates are a good start, my concern is that FEMA was too broad in its approach. The EOP it designed is meant to encompass *all* emergency situations including what to do in the case of fire, severe weather, earthquake, pandemic or mass shooting. While some commonality is going to exist between various disaster scenarios (such as contacting emergency services), it's fair to say that the methods of protecting, preventing, mitigating, responding to and recovering from a mass shooting will be entirely different from protecting, preventing, mitigating, responding to and recovering from a pandemic. Here, I'll combine the guidelines and recommendations established by FEMA and supplementing those with my recommendations for creating an EOP specific to mass shootings.

■ *FEMA released this "Guide for Developing High-Quality Emergency Operations Plans for Houses of Worship" in June of 2013. While the guide is successful in highlighting many characteristics unique to houses of worship, it spends just 10 pages specifically looking at EOP guidelines for mass shooting incidents.*

Guide for Developing High-Quality Emergency Operations Plans for Houses of Worship

June 2013

FEMA

TABLE 1.0 GOALS OF THE DETERRENCE MISSION	
Goal 1.1	Present a "say something" campaign to all classrooms.
Goal 1.2	Investigate social media for any student considered "at risk."
Goal 1.3	Create an ability for students to confidentially alert school officials to a potential threat.
Goal 1.4	Determine to what extent any new security measures should be publicly announced.

KEY MISSION AREAS

While PPD-8 and the FEMA guidelines are very broad, they do a good job in suggesting a number of key mission areas that should be considered when developing an EOP. FEMA's mission areas include: protecting, preventing, mitigating, responding and recovering. For our purposes, I'll revise those five mission areas outlined by FEMA into four mission areas, including deterrence, protection, response and mitigation. Let's first review a quick summary of what should be considered within each of those mission areas.

Deterrence

In this context, deterrence means the capabilities necessary to avoid, prevent or stop a threatened or real mass shooting before it occurs. Those capabilities might include a program designed to uncover threats before they materialize, such as creating an educational program, or it might include a process to review the social media accounts of "at-risk" individuals. It might include implementing overt physical security measures designed to deter a mass shooter from ever considering your house of worship, school or business as a target. Think of the deterrence mission as everything that is done to prevent an attack from ever occurring in the first place.

Protection

Protection will include all of the physical and procedural capabilities designed to stop or inhibit a mass shooter from successfully carrying out his plans if your institution is targeted. Those capabilities may include hardening the physical structure of your institution or installing active countermeasures. It may include a procedural response such as an enhanced lockdown or designating specific rooms as protected safe rooms, pre-staged with certain equipment. And it may include designating and training staff members or volunteers for an armed response. Think of the protection mission as a defensive plan which will include everything that is built, installed, implemented or planned before an attack ever occurs that will help you respond to the attack once it is launched.

Response

In this context, response means how individuals, staff members and those in leadership or assigned positions should respond to a mass shooter making entry into your house of worship, school or business. That response may include the immediate implementation of the lockdown procedures and the active countermeasures detailed under the protection mission. It may include

■ Similar to the guide designed for houses of worship, FEMA also created a template designed to meet the specific needs of schools called the Guide for Developing High-Quality School Emergency Operations Plans.

TABLE 2.0 GOALS OF THE PROTECTION MISSION	
Goal 2.1	Prevent unauthorized access through all school entrances and classroom doors.
Goal 2.2	Reduce the ability for intruders to force entry into exterior and interior doors.
Goal 2.3	Provide immediate visual identification of visitors and intruders.
Goal 2.4	Improve ability for staff and students to safely shelter in place.
Goal 2.5	Decentralize authorization for initiating lockdown.
Goal 2.6	Reduce or eliminate an intruder's ability to advance into classroom areas unimpeded.
Goal 2.7	Provide the ability to stop an intruder with force if necessary.
Goal 2.8	Create a system or procedure to automatically alert law enforcement when a lockdown has been called.

an immediate or automated communication with law enforcement. It may include an immediate response by individuals to run, hide or fight. It may include the activation of on-scene armed responders using the procedures also outlined in the protection mission. Think of the response mission as everything that should occur *during* an attack. If you think of the protection mission as the defensive plan, the response mission could be thought of as the offensive plan, or as the "playbook" that is put into action if an attack occurs.

Mitigation

In this context, mitigation refers to a plan designed to mitigate the loss of life when an attack has occurred.

This might be done through the implementation of a triage system and through emergency first-aid treatment of victims by on-scene personnel before emergency services arrives on the scene. Think of the mitigation mission as everything that has been prepared in advance to minimize the number of casualties if an attack does occur.

It may be obvious that each of the mission areas outlined are intertwined. For example, the greater the amount of protection implemented at a house of worship, school or business, the greater the chances that a mass shooter will be deterred from ever targeting that location in the first place. As an example, imagine how the attacker's thinking may have changed if Sandy Hook Elementary School had publicly announced a set of revolutionary security measures, including a sophisticated lockdown procedure initiated by any staff member using a fob. Or if there had been hardened school entrances with video surveillance rather than the existing glass entrance, auto-locking doors on all classrooms and active countermeasures, including ceiling-mounted fog cannons outside of each classroom and armed staff members. It's unlikely that his planning would have changed to defeat those multiple layers of security. Instead, he most likely would have given up his plan entirely. By the way, if you think the security measures that I just mentioned are pure science fiction, you'll read in a moment about how those exact measures are being implemented today.

Intertwined relationships occur between other primary mission areas, including between response and mitigation. For example, as part of the response mission, if you've developed a plan to teach and practice the "Run, Hide, Fight" methodology, then you'll also mitigate the number of victims needing critical care in the immediate aftermath. My suggestion is that you not get hung up on debating under which mission a particular topic should fall. Just document it under whichever mission feels most appropriate. Even with that advice, if you're still finding yourself bogged down in the details, you can simplify your mission list into three buckets rather than four. For example:

- What plans should be put in place that can prevent an attack before it occurs?
- What plans should be put in place that will counter the threat during an attack?

- What plans should be put in place to minimize the loss of life after an attack has occurred?

If the "before, during and after" method of bucketing items works better for your institution, my suggestion is to use that instead.

BEFORE GETTING STARTED

If your institution is ready to develop an Emergency Operations Plan, there are a number of key principles that can help to ensure its successful development. Many organizations never pass the planning stage, and the following advice from FEMA can help to avoid that pitfall. Once again, I will combine advice from FEMA with my own recommendations so that it applies specifically to the topic of mass shooters.

Support by Leadership and Stakeholders

When beginning the process of developing a mass shooter EOP, planning should have broad support within the institution. While a core planning team should be developed to include leaders from your house of worship, school or business, key stakeholders must also be included to ultimately make a plan successful. That doesn't mean that a plan must be developed by the democratic process or that every decision point needs to be voted on by dozens of stakeholders. It does mean that a plan will only be successful if it is supported at the top and supported by anyone who can ultimately cause the plan to fail. And go into this planning knowing that you will be unlikely to gain a unanimous agreement on all

TABLE 3.0 GOALS OF THE RESPONSE MISSION	
Goal 3.1	Implement "Run, Hide, Fight" or a similar program.
Goal 3.2	Implement some level of active countermeasures for use during an attack, such as those implemented at Southwestern High School in Indiana.
Goal 3.3	Implement some level of armed responders on scene, either using live or Simunition® firearms.

aspects of a plan. For example, if part of your plan at your house of worship is to identify all church members who are full-time or part-time law enforcement officers in order to ensure that there are always armed responders on-site, you may find that certain stakeholders simply can't wrap their heads around having guns in a place of worship (or in a school or a business). But rather than allowing your planning process to grind to a halt or rejecting an idea simply because one or two stakeholders are opposed to it, those in leadership positions must make the final determination as to what is in and what is out of the plan, or ultimately, who is on and who is off of the planning committee.

Plan for All Settings and All Times

It's also important to remember that a mass shooter threat can affect a house of worship, school or business at non-standard times and in non-standard locations. For example, it's obvious to plan for what to do when your house of worship is holding a service or when school is in session and all students are in their classrooms. But planning and live drills must also include off-hour events such as when a meeting is being held at night

at the house of worship, when students are in the gym or lunchroom or when they are entering or exiting the school. A "one-size-fits-all" plan will not work.

STEPS TO DEVELOP THE PLAN

A number of steps are involved in successfully developing an EOP:

Step 1: Form a Collaborative Planning Team

The core planning team should include representatives from the institution including leadership and key stakeholders, as well as representation from your community's law enforcement and EMS agencies. When developing a team, my recommendation is to keep the core team to no more than five to seven participants. Those participants can include:

- **1 – 2 leadership representatives.** It isn't required that the senior leader of the institution be on the team, but it will aid in the decision-making process if the leader's representative on the team carries a significant amount of decision-making ability. At a school, this might include a school board member and the principal or assistant principal. At a house of worship, this might include the senior cleric or his representative. At a business, this might include the owner, the president or the individual responsible for security.

- **1 – 2 key stakeholder representatives.** At a school, this might include two teachers or a teacher and a parent. At a house of worship, this might include a senior greeter or usher and a respected congregant. At a business, this might include one or two department managers.

- **1 – 2 local law enforcement and EMS agency representatives.** These individuals should not be required to attend all planning sessions but should be invited at key decision points. I will add here that my recommendation is that you invite these individuals as a courtesy and to gain their subject matter expertise but do not allow these individuals to hold veto power over any of your decisions. For example, if your local law enforcement representative strongly recommends against including an armed response as part of your protection mission, you will ultimately need to decide for your own institution whether that is good advice or bad advice.

- **1 – 2 subject matter experts from within the institution or within the local community if the institution lacks appropriate experts.** These subject matter experts may be active or retired law enforcement officers from within your house of

worship's congregation. They may be active, reserve or retired military personnel from within your house of worship, school or business. They may be individuals with advanced security, emergency first-aid, law enforcement, firearms or other pertinent expertise.

Step 2: Determine Goals and Objectives

As with all planning, creating an EOP must begin with the end goals in mind. For our purposes, goals are defined as broad, general statements that indicate the desired outcome in response to the threat. As explained by FEMA, "Goals are what personnel and other resources are supposed to achieve. Goals also help identify when major activities are complete and what defines a successful outcome." The planning team should develop at least three goals for addressing each of the key mission areas of deterrence, protection, response and mitigation. To give you an example of how this step might be accomplished, I've shown four sample tables in this section for each of the four mission areas. My sample tables outline the goals for each of the mission areas for a hypothetical school, but your goals might be very similar, even if your plan is being developed for a house of worship or a public or private business.

At this step, it will be easy to confuse goals with solutions, and that's actually okay. For example, on the sample table shown on the opposite page, *Table 4.0 Goals of the Mitigation Mission*, from goal 4.4, it would be an obvious next step to say that to achieve this goal, we're going to need to provide emergency first-aid training to teachers, staff members and students. But

TABLE 4.0 GOALS OF THE MITIGATION MISSION	
Goal 4.1	Implement a solution to allow locked-down classrooms to alert responders to the current condition and emergency needs. This will help to mitigate loss of life by directing responders to the locations that need immediate emergency care.
Goal 4.2	Initiate a triage system within each safe zone to allow for victims to be prioritized and treated accordingly.
Goal 4.3	Provide classrooms and other locations with life-saving emergency first-aid supplies. This will help to mitigate the loss of life by providing the tools to allow life-saving treatment for injured victims prior to the arrival of EMS.
Goal 4.4	Provide emergency medical care to victims injured during a mass shooting, using trained or semi-trained staff members and students.

we'll want to ensure that we don't just end our planning by stating the goal and a one- or two- sentence course of action. If the goal is to, "Provide emergency medical care to victims injured during a mass shooting, using trained or semi-trained staff members and students," then the course of action to achieve that goal must be spelled out in much greater detail than simply saying, "We will provide emergency first-aid training to teachers, staff members and students." The full course of action will need to explain what the training will be, who will do it, what products will be needed, what the cost will be, etc. That detail gets fleshed out in Step 3.

Step 3: Detailing Courses of Action

As explained by FEMA, courses of action will address the what, who, when, where and why. During this step, the planning team will develop proposed or possible courses of action to achieve each goal outlined in Step 2. While doing this, the planning team may evolve or add to the goals based upon new information developed during this step. For example, new technology may be discovered that was previously unknown, or subject matter expertise within your house of worship, school or business may be uncovered during this step. You may also discover that certain goals can be combined or more than one goal can be achieved by a particular course of action.

During this step, planners will develop potential courses of action to achieve goals by answering the following questions:

- What is the proposed course of action?
- Who is responsible for researching, planning and developing the action? For example, if training is required to institute the course of action, who is

responsible for developing the training plan? Who is responsible for conducting the training? Who will attend the training? If a technology solution is required, such as implementing video security at all entrances, who will research solutions, will decide on a solution, pay for the solution, install the solution and conduct maintenance on the solution?

- Who is responsible for conducting the course of action? In other words, who will complete the course of action during an actual mass shooter threat?
- What resources, tools and skills are needed to perform the action?
- What are the pros, cons, risks and costs associated with implementing this course of action?

As you can see on the sample *Course of Action* table on the opposite page, it's helpful to have a consistent numbering system to keep your missions, goals and courses of action organized. For example, on our sample tables, the numbering system lets everyone know that goal 4.3 is the third goal of the mitigation mission.

After your course of action tables are completed, members of the planning committee will compare the costs, benefits, timeliness and feasibility of each proposed course of action against the goals. Based upon this comparison, planners will select the preferred course or courses of action to move forward in the planning process.

Step 4: Conduct Tabletop Exercises

Prior to the actual implementation of any course of action, the planning team should conduct tabletop exercises that walk through a variety of mass shooting scenarios to determine whether the course of action meets the goal stated in Step 2. This activity will help to assess the plan and resources and will help to determine if any holes in the plan exist. A tabletop exercise is simple, usually conducted on a whiteboard (even though it's called a "tabletop" exercise) that walks through a variety of scenarios. As one or more individuals verbally walks through a scenario and outlines it on the whiteboard, other team members can ask questions which will help to identify any gaps in the plan. For example, if you've reached the part in a scenario where trained or semi-trained staff members and students will need to provide emergency first aid to injured victims, you might quickly discover that you've included in your plan a course of action to pre-stage emergency first-aid equipment in classrooms but neglected to consider pre-staging the same equipment in the front office or in conference rooms that have been designated as safe rooms.

Step 5: Conduct a Live Walk-Through

After conducting a number of tabletop exercises, the planning team should conduct a live, practical exercise that walks through a mass shooting scenario to once again determine if each course of action meets the goals outlined in Step 2. This walk-through will require additional participation of volunteers to find any gaps within the plan. As an example of a weakness that might be discovered during a walk-through, let's say that your house of worship has included a course of action for congregants to move into designated conference rooms or classrooms and lock the doors when a lockdown

PROPOSED COURSES OF ACTION FOR MITIGATION GOAL 4.3

Goal 4.3: Provide emergency medical care to victims injured during a mass shooting using trained or semi-trained staff members and students.

4.3.1: What is the proposed course of action?	Provide emergency first-aid training to all full-time and part-time staff members.
4.3.2: Who is responsible for instituting the action?	Training will be developed by [subject matter expert] in conjunction with local EMS support. Initial training will consist of 16 hours of lecture and hands-on practical exercises. A 4-hour refresher training will be held annually. Training will include advanced instruction on how to implement a triage, how to stop severe bleeding, including the use of commercial and field expedient tourniquets, how to treat penetrating chest and abdominal injuries, and how to treat for shock.
4.3.3: Who is responsible for conducting the course of action?	In the event of a mass shooting, the senior staff member present will institute an emergency triage and emergency first-aid treatment of victims will be the responsibility of all staff members certified in the course outlined above.
4.3.4: What resources, tools and skills are needed to perform the action?	Equipment for use during training and equipment to be stocked in each classroom and staff room will include: commercial tourniquet, commercial chest seals, compressed gauze, trauma pad, nasal airways in multiple sizes and a blanket. May consider commercially available trauma kit for classroom use.
4.3.5: What are the pros, cons or risks associated with implementing this course of action?	**Pros:** Emergency care can begin within the 4- to 5-minute window where severe bleeding, a penetrating chest injury or a compromised airway may cause the death of the victim. **Cons:** This could open up the school to litigation if treatment were to be performed by a non-professional rescuer. **Risks:** No known risks other than the issue of litigation. **Cost:** Initial equipment and training costs estimated to be $8,000, annual cost estimated to be $1,000.

is called. (This course of action would fall under the Response Mission). But during a walk-through exercise, you might discover the following weaknesses:

- Several conference rooms designated as "safe rooms" lack locks or require that a key be used, and your plan didn't account for this.
- Several of the rooms have doors with viewports, and you didn't consider how to mark areas in the room that are out of the line of sight (and the line of fire) from an attacker peering in through the door's viewport.

If those weaknesses were discovered during a walk-through, it doesn't mean that the course of action should be completely discarded, but it does mean that your course of action will need to be revised, such as adding locks to doors that need them (locks that don't require a key) or adding a taped line on the floor to identify which areas are inside and outside of the line of sight from the door's viewport. It might even cause you to reconsider which rooms you will consider safe rooms in the first place. I'll add that it's extremely important to not skip this or the next step and simply end your planning process after doing a tabletop exercise. It's these walk-throughs and the full-scale exercises that we'll discuss in Step 6 that will find the holes in your plan which could ultimately cost lives. In other words, you won't discover that a room lacks locks or requires a key to lock it while sitting at a conference room table, and you don't want to discover it when a disaster is unfolding around you.

Step 6: Conduct a Full-Scale Exercise

While a tabletop exercise and a walk-through of your plan will help to revise the plan and make it better, after your courses of action have been fully developed and implemented, it's critical to conduct a full-scale exercise involving all team members outlined in your plan. While FEMA recommends that a full-scale exercise include emergency management, law enforcement and EMS personnel, it's my recommendation that you conduct at least one full-scale exercise without involving those agencies. While that might sound counterintuitive, my reason for suggesting this is that if you do include those agencies on your first full-scale exercise, the exercise is more likely to become about *their* response to a mass shooting rather than *your* response. For example, if you haven't run a full-scale exercise to test out how you would implement a triage system, your local EMS agency is most likely to respond, "Don't worry about setting up a triage, we'll take care of that." If you haven't run a full-scale exercise to test out how you would use on-scene armed responders, your local law enforcement agency is most likely to respond, "Don't worry about an armed response. You guys should just go to your safe rooms and we'll take care of an armed response." Keep in mind that the EOP you are developing is not to outline how law enforcement or EMS will respond to a mass shooting. Your EOP is designed to outline how your employees or staff members and your students or congregants will respond in order to survive the eight to nine minutes (or longer) it will take for the shooting to end. If triage and treatment of life-threatening injuries has not started until after the shooting has ended,

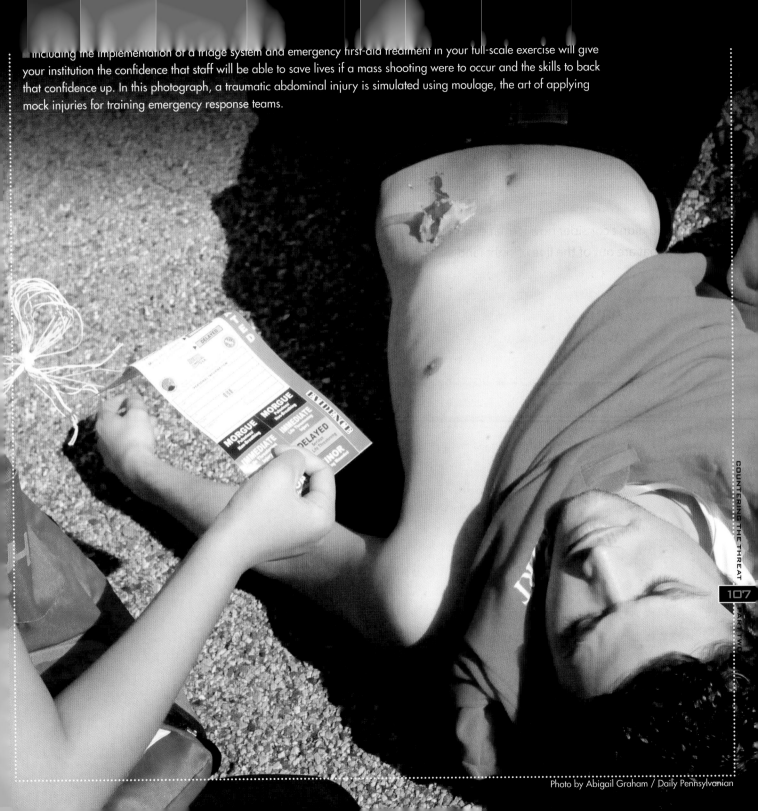

Including the implementation of a triage system and emergency first-aid treatment in your full-scale exercise will give your institution the confidence that staff will be able to save lives if a mass shooting were to occur and the skills to back that confidence up. In this photograph, a traumatic abdominal injury is simulated using moulage, the art of applying mock injuries for training emergency response teams.

you will lose lives. If an armed response is immediately launched rather than nine minutes into the shooting, you will save lives. So my advice is to run at least one full-scale exercise within your own institution prior to running FEMA's version of a full-scale exercise, which they describe as, "multi-agency, multi-jurisdiction efforts in which resources are deployed. This type of exercise tests collaboration among the agencies and participants, public information systems, communications systems, and equipment."

I'll add that when you conduct a walk-through (Step 5) and a full-scale exercise (Step 6), it's easy to fall into the trap of making your scenario fit your plan. For example, if your plan only accounts for an attacker entering through the front door, don't just run a walk-through or full-scale exercise of a mock attacker entering through the front door. The walk-through and full-scale exercises are meant to find holes in the plan, not to make everyone feel good about all the hard work they've put into it. Nothing will educate you better than failure, and it's far better to find the failure during an exercise than to find it in real life.

Step 7: Review, Revise, Maintain and Train the Plan

If you've done your tabletop and walk-through exercises carefully, your full-scale exercise should primarily find holes in training, tactics or strategy, rather than holes in the physical implementation of courses of action designed to fulfill the primary missions. As FEMA explains it, "Planning is a continuous process that does not stop when the plan is published."

Lastly, if you've only documented your plan but you haven't *trained* to the plan, you're still left with a gaping hole if a mass shooting does occur. As discussed in the section on developing courses of action, a training plan is an incredibly important part of your course of action, since it will dictate exactly what all parties should know and do, as well as give them a chance to practice and perfect their part of the plan. As an example, if your plan has rewritten the procedures for what should occur when a lockdown is initiated at your school, but you haven't trained teachers and students on those new procedures, then nothing has really changed. Like first-aid and CPR education, training to your plan cannot be considered "one and done." Minimal training should be held at all levels of the organization annually, and at least monthly for large-scale procedures like lockdown drills.

While this section was meant to provide you with a framework on the procedures for creating an Emergency Operations Plan for your institution, in the next several sections I'll be reviewing in greater detail a number of specific considerations, goals and courses of action you should consider when developing an EOP for your own school, house of worship or business.

While you should eventually include emergency management, law enforcement and EMS personnel, you should first run at least one full-scale exercise without those agencies. If they're included in the first full-scale exercise, the exercise will most likely become about their response rather than your response. Remember, your EOP must include a plan on how to prevent an attack in the first place or end it early and save lives if an attack does occur. That means surviving at least nine minutes on your own, without those agencies to assist.

Photo by Amy Voigt / Toledo Blade

SPECIAL CONSIDERATIONS FOR SCHOOLS

Let's face it — the security at most of our nation's schools is not just poor; it's abysmal. It's years after attacks on Sandy Hook and Virginia Tech, and our schools remain as unprotected as they were in the days and months leading up to those tragedies.

In this section, I'm going to get specific on a number of security measures that will dramatically improve the safety and security of our nation's schools, inside and out. We'll look at the proper way to secure school entrances, how to harden classroom and staff room doors, how to improve lockdown procedures and even how to implement active countermeasures. But before we jump into those details though, let's first take a look at a school in Indiana that is a model for what school security should be. It is easily the safest and most secure school in the nation.

A MODEL OF SCHOOL SECURITY

In the aftermath of Sandy Hook, as state legislatures across the country debated magazine capacity, the Indiana Sheriffs' Association (ISA) chose to ignore that red herring and instead got to work on developing a new

model of school security. ISA picked Southwestern High School in rural Shelby County to serve as the prototype. During the research phase of the project, a partnership was initiated with the Virginia-based company Net Talon, whose solution, Virtual Command, seemed to be just what the sheriffs' association was looking for. In a nutshell, Virtual Command combines real-time intelligence-gathering capabilities with physical obstacles and active countermeasures to take the power away from mass shooters and put it back into the hands of the individuals responsible for keeping our kids safe. Don Jones, the president and co-founder of Net Talon, knows a thing or two about being shot at, after having served as an Army Ranger and second lieutenant during the peak of the Vietnam war in 1968 to 1969. As Jones explains it, "Virtual Command gives law enforcement command and control, when today they have none."

As Jones sees it, the mass shootings at Columbine, Virginia Tech, Red Lake and Sandy Hook all had two things in common. First, the physical protection for students and staff was woefully inadequate. At each of those locations, the inner and outer doors of the buildings were unsecure or utilized security methods that were easily breached or difficult to activate under stress. The classroom doors at Virginia Tech lacked even the most basic locks, and the students and professors were forced to block the doors with their hands and feet, many of them dying in the process. At Sandy Hook, the glass "security entrance" might have been good for appearances but was easily breached, as the perpetrator shot his way through it. The classroom doors at Sandy Hook had their own point of failure, requiring that the doors be locked using a key rather than a standard deadbolt or self-locking unit. In the aftermath, it was discovered that all of the classroom doors were locked except for classrooms eight and ten, the two classrooms where Lanza murdered the majority of his victims. Tragically, keys were found on the floor next to one of the murdered teachers.

The second common thread that runs through not just school shootings but all mass shootings is that once the shooter has entered his target building, it's

■ Security begins at the outer doors, with each of the school entrances secured with steel hardened doors, combined with a video surveillance system so that administrators can tell who is at the door before granting or denying them access.

the shooter that has control of the situation, while potential victims and responders operate in the blind as to the shooter's location, his direction of travel, his weapons capabilities and of the location of any victims needing care.

Hardening Up

The Virtual Command solution solves those issues and more, starting at the outer doors. As implemented at Southwestern High School, each of the school entrances are now secured with steel-hardened doors, combined with a video surveillance system so that administrators can tell who is at the door before granting or denying them access. If an intruder were able to breach this first line of defense, any teacher or staff member can now initiate a lockdown by way of a key fob that can be pressed at the first sign of trouble. At Sandy Hook, lockdowns could only be called by the front office. That opportunity died when principal Dawn Hochsprung was gunned down before she could raise the alarm. Pressing the fob not only initiates a school lockdown across the entire campus, announced by sirens and flashing lights, it also automatically locks the ballistically protected office door and immediately alerts the sheriff's office that a lockdown has been called. As observed by Deputy Sheriff Mike Kersey of the Montgomery County Sheriff's Department, "On average, it takes two to four minutes after a shooting has begun before a call is made to 911 as victims are rapidly retreating to a safe location or are fighting off the attacker." Considering that most

mass shootings last just eight to nine minutes, shaving two to four minutes off of law enforcement response time will end the attack early, ultimately saving lives.

The other major obstacle Virtual Command addresses is the fact that in all previous mass shootings, armed responders must formulate a response with almost no information about the shooter's position as they arrive on scene and prepare to make entry. In the case of Southwestern High School, the sheriff's office will instantly know where the shooter is, what weapons he's carrying and the location of any victims through the use of dozens of cameras and motion detectors situated throughout the school. These are all accessible in real-time at the command center in the sheriff's office. As explained by Deputy Kersey, "We can locate him. We can get a description of him immediately. We can track him throughout the building. We'll know his weapons platform. We'll know what he's doing and where he's doing it instantly." SWAT team commander Brian Chesterson added, "It takes the guesswork out of everything. Once we arrive on a scene, it's 20 seconds to an end."

Initiating a lockdown won't just set the sheriff's office into motion, it will also initiate an orchestrated response by the school's students and staff. Upon hearing the lockdown sirens, all teachers and students are trained to immediately enter their classrooms, where a self-locking, bullet-resistant door secures the students and teacher. While most typical classroom doors can be breached with the appropriate tools or a gunshot to the window, Southwestern's doors are protected by hardened steel designed to resist even high-caliber rounds. The doors also have enhanced and hardened hinges and locking systems and "ballistically protected" viewports which, during testing, were able to defeat cartridges as heavy as .44 Magnum and shotgun blasts of 00 buckshot. The testing didn't stop there. After being fired upon, the doors were then attacked with a fire ax, where they continued to hold even after more than 70 hits.

As we've discussed, these attackers will typically not spend more than a few seconds trying to gain access to any given room, quickly moving on to find an easier

target if access is blocked. These doors will do more than just frustrate an attacker. They will save the life of every child and staff member who makes it to the safe side of the door. But rather than just waiting passively behind the door, students and teachers are taught to immediately position themselves on the far side of a red line of tape on the floor, which puts them out of the line of sight (and the line of fire) from an attacker peering in through the door's viewport. In a demonstration shown on NBC's *Today Show*, the students had positioned themselves on the far side of the red line within seconds, where they stacked desks into a barrier wall. They then sat on the floor with their knees up to protect their internal organs, holding a thick textbook in front of their heads. While desks and textbooks might not be considered adequate to stop a bullet, those desks and textbooks will make great defensive weapons if a shooter ever did make it into the classroom. We'll discuss more about this in the section on "Run, Hide, Fight".

Real-Time Intelligence

The Virtual Command solution at Southwestern High School allows law enforcement officers to gather real-time intelligence through the use of dozens of cameras and motion detectors mounted throughout the school. As explained by SWAT team commander Brian Chesterson, "It takes the guesswork out of everything. Once we arrive on a scene, it's 20 seconds to an end."

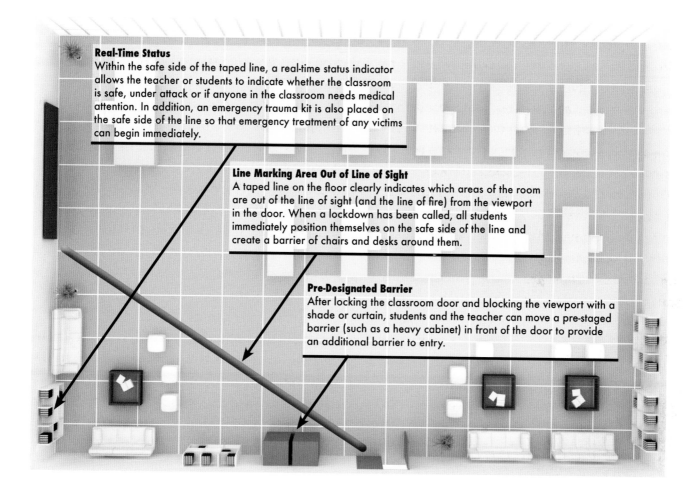

Real-Time Status
Within the safe side of the taped line, a real-time status indicator allows the teacher or students to indicate whether the classroom is safe, under attack or if anyone in the classroom needs medical attention. In addition, an emergency trauma kit is also placed on the safe side of the line so that emergency treatment of any victims can begin immediately.

Line Marking Area Out of Line of Sight
A taped line on the floor clearly indicates which areas of the room are out of the line of sight (and the line of fire) from the viewport in the door. When a lockdown has been called, all students immediately position themselves on the safe side of the line and create a barrier of chairs and desks around them.

Pre-Designated Barrier
After locking the classroom door and blocking the viewport with a shade or curtain, students and the teacher can move a pre-staged barrier (such as a heavy cabinet) in front of the door to provide an additional barrier to entry.

At Virginia Tech and Columbine, more than one victim died because responders had no way of knowing where the injured victims were and whether the shooter was still an active threat. The Virtual Command solution helps to address that problem by placing a box inside each classroom where the teacher can toggle a switch indicating "All Safe," "Under Attack" or "Need Medical Attention." This information will also be relayed to the sheriff's command center, which can then send that information to armed responders or EMS personnel. Speaking of a medical response, each classroom is also supplied with an emergency trauma-aid kit including a tourniquet and compression bandages, which can save lives when the injured re waiting for the professionals to make entry. We'll also address that topic in the "Triage and Treat the Wounded" section. If those features and capabilities sound impressive, you haven't yet heard the best part.

Disorient and Disrupt

Other than the sound of the attacker's gunfire and the cries of his victims, mass casualty attack survivors have described the scenes as being eerily quiet. That silence works in the shooter's favor as he moves from room to room, seeking out more victims and listening closely for the impending law enforcement response. The Virtual Command solution at Southwestern High takes away that advantage by providing an ability to disorient and disrupt the shooter using countermeasures worthy of a James Bond thriller. Since the location of the shooter can be determined with pinpoint accuracy at any given moment during an attack, responders operating from miles away at the command center can launch a series of countermeasures positioned outside of every classroom door, including blinding strobe lights, deafening sirens and even ceiling-mounted smoke cannons. This creates what Net Talon describes as a "hot zone" around the shooter while all other hallways remain clear for responders. This hot zone is designed to disorient the shooter and disrupt his momentum, forcing him away from any door he may be trying to breach. Once launched, the countermeasures also close the school's fire doors, which are secured with one-way locks. That means that once the shooter leaves any hallway containing classrooms, not only can he not re-enter that hallway, he is also locked out from all other hallways containing classrooms.

Keep in mind that these countermeasures don't need to delay a shooter for hours. They only need to delay the shooter for the short period of time required to ensure that all classroom doors are secured and buy law enforcement precious minutes while they prepare their response. More than 70 percent of school shooters commit suicide in place when one of two things happen: they run out of victims or they believe that law enforcement is about to make entry. The combination of hardened doors, pinpoint intelligence and active countermeasures will make any shooter foolish enough to enter Southwestern High believe that both of those events have occurred, and the attack may end without a single fatality other than the shooter. I think most of us could live with that.

The Cost

The cost of the system? About $400,000 at Southwestern, which was covered by a combination of government grants and money donated by a local security company. School Superintendent Paula Maurer summed up those costs with this statement: "If schools can afford to pay for football fields, stadiums and computers, they can find the money for security." While Southwestern was the prototype, Indiana House Bill 491 would make paying for these systems easier across all of Indiana by authorizing schools to charge a safety fee of up to $20 per student per year, plus a public safety fee tacked onto local property taxes not to exceed $10 per month. The bill would also provide state-matching funds for any school implementing a system, up to $125,000. One version of the bill even makes these systems mandatory across every public school and state college across Indiana.

 The cost of the system ran about $400,000 at Southwestern, which was covered by a combination of government grants and money donated by a local security company. School Superintendent Paula Maurer summed up those costs with this statement: "If schools can afford to pay for football fields, stadiums and computers, they can find the money for security." On a side note, the average cost for a high school football stadium is now $6 million, with many high school stadiums exceeding $25 million, and the most expensive high school football stadium in history costing in excess of $70 million. Who says we don't have enough money to implement adequate school security?

While you might be concerned that Southwestern High has defeated the purpose by being so public with their school security measures, thereby allowing a potential mass shooter to figure out how he would defeat them, I'd argue the opposite is true. Mass shooters don't want to be known for defeating sophisticated multilayered security. They want to go down in history for body count. In every mass shooting that we profiled in Part One, the mass shooter simply walked into the target zone and started shooting. No history exists of a mass shooter fighting his way through hardened security or past sophisticated countermeasures and armed personnel. None. By being so public with Southwestern High's enhanced security systems, school and law enforcement officials have very likely ensured that the school will never become a target in the first place. In other words, as part of the Protect and Respond EOP Missions, they dramatically improved their Deter Mission as well.

School Security Checklist

Now that we've looked at a model for what school security should be, let's turn that into a school security checklist to discuss and consider when developing an EOP for your own school. The following school security checklist should be used when evaluating your school's current security, as well as to develop what courses of action should be selected for your EOP.

Outer Doors

- All outer doors must be secured so that visitors need to be be cleared before entering the school. This may be done with a secured exterior door and video check-in system or through an interior security door and a "sterile area" between the outer and inner doors. All visitors must be funneled through these secure entrances with no ability to bypass them.
- Doors, windows and hinges must be ballistically protected. In other words, the doors and windows must be able to withstand gunshots and other methods of breaching.
- Students and staff must be trained to avoid "drafting", or an individual who has not been cleared following a cleared individual through the security door.

Classroom Doors

- All doors must have a deadbolt or auto-locking mechanism that can be secured quickly with no key.
- Doors should have a backup lock such as a hotel-style throw over lock, *Door Jammer* or similar security doorstop.
- All classroom doors, windows and hinges must be ballistically protected.
- Doors must be rated to withstand at least 10 minutes of forced entry.
- Shades or curtains must be pre-installed to quickly and completely block door viewports.

Lockdown Procedures

- A decentralized ability to initiate a lockdown must be implemented, such as providing security key fobs to all teachers. When pressed, these will initiate the lockdown. Training must be updated so that teachers understand their authority to initiate a lockdown if they hear what they believe to be gunfire or see an intruder.

- When a lockdown is initiated, the system must automatically call law enforcement rather than requiring a 911 call be made. As mentioned, the average delay to call 911 at mass shootings is two minutes. If we look at the nation's five worst school shootings, four students and teachers died every two minutes. If we end the mass shooting two minutes early, we will save lives.

- Students and staff should be alerted to the lockdown by audible sirens and flashing lights. At universities and colleges, procedures must be put in place and practiced to use social media, including Twitter and Facebook, to announce the lockdown, directing students and staff to initiate the procedures they've been trained on, including implementation of "Run, Hide, Fight."

- Advanced systems should provide law enforcement with a picture of what's occurring within the school through video access to the interior and exterior of the school. See the case study of Southwestern High for more information.

- All rooms designated as safe rooms, including classrooms, should have a taped line on the floor indicating which areas are inside or outside of the field of view from the door's viewport.

- All classrooms, staff rooms, conference rooms and offices should have an intercom tied into law enforcement channels to indicate the status of the room's occupants (all safe, under attack or medical assistance needed).

- All classrooms, staff rooms, conference rooms and offices must have emergency first-aid supplies, and students and staff must be trained in their use.

Active Countermeasures

- All classrooms must have barricades that can be quickly pushed or dropped in front of the door, such as moveable cabinets or bookcases. As part of lockdown drill training, specific students should be preassigned to immediately move these barricades when a lockdown has been called and all students are behind the secured classroom door.

- Advanced systems should include other active countermeasures such as sirens, strobe lights or fog cannons to disorient and disrupt the attacker.

- All teachers, staff members and students must be drilled on the "Run, Hide Fight" methodology, including training them to fight back with improvised weapons if no other option exists.

- As part of your school's EOP, you must consider including armed and trained personnel on the property equipped with live or Simunition firearms.

WHAT TEACHERS SHOULD KNOW

Lockdown drills must not only be procedurally correct, they must also be fast. How fast? A good test for every teacher in every school would be to see how quickly a healthy runner can sprint from the closest school entrance to your classroom. If that can be done in five seconds, then you have four seconds to get your students into the classroom and secure the door. Self-locking doors, or at a minimum, doors with standard deadbolt locks are an absolute must for every classroom door in the country.

During lockdown drills, students must also be taught to do more than simply huddle on one side of the classroom. Instead, they must be taught to fight back — and fight back *aggressively* — if a shooter enters their classroom. During lockdown drills, schools must implement or teachers can improvise counterattack plans by instructing students to pick up any object and hold it back in a "thrower's stance," preparing for an attacker to make entry. For younger kids, the object might be a book, a stapler, their shoes or a glue stick. Older students should be taught to pick up chairs or other heavier objects. Any object thrown at an attacker will break his momentum, which may cause him to back out of the classroom. Simulated counterattacks can even be practiced by providing students with soft rubber objects that can be thrown at mock attackers making entry through the classroom door.

Not only would that type of exercise make lockdown drills less frightening, it would also begin to build the proper neural pathways that fighting back is okay, necessary and expected. From junior high through college, students should be taught to defend and attack as a team by immediately locking the door and barricading it with the designated cabinet or bookshelf, then striking the shooter with hardened objects to the head and torso if he makes entry.

If you are a teacher and your school has not yet implemented an armed educator program, you'll need to include a baseball bat or other incapacitating tool in your classroom. If a shooter enters your classroom, you not only have the legal right but the moral obligation to use deadly force to stop him. Huddling with your kids on one side of the classroom, whispering to them, "Everything is going to be okay," is not living up to that obligation.

While the defensive measures included on the checklist or those implemented at Southwestern High might sound ineffective since a determined attacker could still possibly be able to eventually breach a locked door, remember that mass shooters know that they'll have just nine to ten minutes to complete their attack before the police will make entry. Delaying a shooter for even one or two minutes is enough to either force the shooter to move on and try a different target or to end his life. The students in classroom 205 at Virginia Tech didn't need to delay the shooter for hours or even minutes. When he was unable to breach the door that students had barricaded with tables, he gave up in seconds and moved back to the classrooms where no such barricades had been erected. If Virginia Tech had installed auto-locking doors, deadbolts or backup locks on the classroom doors, it's very likely that every student in classrooms 204, 207 and 211 would have survived.

WHAT PARENTS SHOULD KNOW

While the majority of planning and practice for what to do in the event of a mass shooting at a school will fall on the shoulders of the school staff and students, parents should also be aware that what they do may also help or hinder their children if the school is targeted. Here are a few suggestions for parents:

- If you are alerted that your child's school is the subject of an attack, *do not* call him or her. If your child's school is in a lockdown and he or she is hiding in either a safe room or an area that is decidedly unsafe, your child's ringing phone might be all the shooter needs to find that hiding spot.

- *Do not* call law enforcement agencies asking for updates. During any mass shooting event, law enforcement officials, including the dispatch center, will be overwhelmed by communication with responders on the scene and the hundreds of others calling in to report a school shooting. Atop that, they'll also be responsible for simultaneously dealing with their standard load of medical, fire and other police response needs. Do not add to the confusion by calling in for an update; instead, allow the process to run its course.

- *Do not* drive to the school looking for an update. Nothing is more frustrating to emergency services personnel than being delayed to a scene because of traffic conditions. If you and other parents are choking the roads or parking lots, you are delaying critical services from ending the attack and providing emergency treatment to the injured. Think about it

this way: How would you feel if the paramedic that will be responsible for saving the life of your child is stuck in traffic behind your vehicle?

- If your child's school is unwilling to commit to implementing "Run, Hide, Fight" or a comparable program, you must take personal responsibility for training your child. For younger children, this might be teaching them that it's okay to run away when they hear the sound of gunfire, or that it's okay to throw *anything* at a bad person in an attempt to escape. For older children, encourage them to discuss the methodology with teachers and other students to determine if they can implement the program in their own classroom, even if other classrooms ignore it.

- If your school board has yet to develop an EOP specific to mass shootings, help be the catalyst to force them to begin the process. Speak with other parents about the idea and share the topics in this book with them. We'll talk a bit more about these grassroots efforts in the summary of the book.

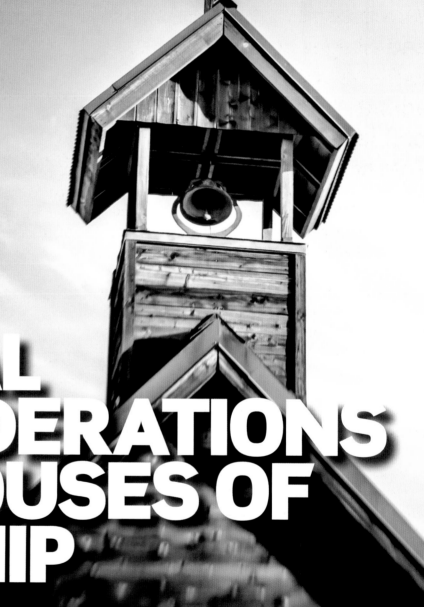

SPECIAL CONSIDERATIONS FOR HOUSES OF WORSHIP

They say that the first step toward recovery is admitting that you have a problem. But in cities, towns and villages across America, we're having a difficult time admitting that we have a problem with church security. That has to change.

We talk of our churches, synagogues, mosques and other places of worship as being "places of sanctuary," and we act surprised whenever a violent attack is perpetuated against one of these locations. We think the fact that we go there to pray to and commune with God will create some kind of magical force field to keep bad things and bad people away. I apologize in advance if my next statement sounds blasphemous, but if an armed attacker enters your place of worship, God is not going to stop him ... but an armed volunteer just might. Or a locked security door, or an escape plan that has been practiced repeatedly by your parishioners. The reality is, it may take all three of those countermeasures to prevent or end an attack.

But houses of worship face different security issues when compared to schools or private businesses. The same "open-door" policy that makes houses of worship welcoming for parishioners and visitors makes an attractive environment for potential mass shooters. Regardless of religious affiliation and mission, houses of worship will always breed a special kind of hatred that is rarely matched. If you are a member of a synagogue or a Christian church there are, at this very moment, any number of Islamic radicals in the U.S. and around the world that dream of burning your house of worship to the ground and killing everyone in it. If you are a member of a mosque, there are demented individuals who may currently be planning to murder your members. If you are a member of a church of color, regardless of your faith, there are individuals who harbor the most vile, disgusting and hateful racial views, leading them to plan and carry out murder in the very place you consider to be a place of sanctuary and safety. This was the case with the attacker who murdered nine parishioners at Emanuel African Methodist Episcopal Church in Charleston simply because they were African-American.

UNIQUE SECURITY CHALLENGES

Security challenges faced by houses of worship include:

- Doors are often unlocked to maintain a welcoming atmosphere for parishioners and visitors.
- An "open-door" policy means that strangers unknown to parishioners and staff will be common.
- Most roles (greeters, ushers, counselors and teachers) are staffed by part-time volunteers.
- Viewing a house of worship as "God's house" can affect strategic thinking when compared to private businesses and schools. For example, the idea of arming security volunteers may "just feel wrong" to

those on the EOP planning committee.

- Because houses of worship consider at least one mission to be peace, it may be difficult to convince the planning committee or religious leaders that "fight" should be included in the "Run, Hide, Fight" program, particularly when it comes to an armed response.

A HOUSE OF WORSHIP SECURITY CHECKLIST

As we did with schools, let's also look at a security checklist that should be discussed and considered when developing an EOP for your house of worship. The following checklist should be used when evaluating your house of worship's current security and used to develop what courses of action should be selected for your EOP.

Outer Doors

While schools can justify treating the entire interior as a "sterile zone" where only approved and authorized individuals may make entry, the mission of houses of worship make that approach much more difficult. However, it is possible to implement the following security to outer doors:

- Visitors should be funneled through a single door or set of doors, with all other doors considered "fire doors." These can be opened from the inside if the building must be evacuated but are locked from the outside.
- Even if you choose to leave the main doors unsecured, a video security system should still be installed.

- Video cameras may also be installed at other entrances. In many cases, the appearance of monitored security may be enough to deter attackers (and, as an added bonus, burglars) from attempting to make entry.

Inner Doors

Because of the "open-door" policy of most houses of worship, the security of inner doors to offices, conference rooms, classrooms, etc. takes on additional importance. As with schools, all inner doors should have the following security capabilities:

- All doors must have a deadbolt or auto-locking mechanism that can be secured quickly with no key.
- Doors should have a back-up lock such as a hotel-style throw-over lock, door-jammer or similar security doorstop.
- All doors, windows and hinges must be ballistically protected.
- Doors must be rated to withstand at least 10 minutes of attempted forced entry.
- Shades or curtains must be pre-installed to quickly and completely block door viewports.

Lockdown Procedures

- As with schools, a decentralized ability to initiate lockdown, such as providing security key fobs to staff members or volunteers, must be implemented.
- When a lockdown is called, the system must automatically call law enforcement.
- Advanced systems should provide law enforcement with a picture of what's occurring within the house of worship through video access to the interior and exterior of the facility.
- All rooms designated as "safe," including classrooms, conference rooms and offices, should have a line marked on the floor indicating which areas are inside or outside of the field of view from the door's viewport.
- All safe rooms should have an intercom tied into law enforcement channels to indicate the status of the room's occupants (all safe, under attack or medical assistance needed).
- All safe rooms must have emergency first-aid supplies, and volunteers and staff must be trained in their use.

Active Countermeasures

While classrooms and staff rooms might lend themselves to the same types of active countermeasures that I reviewed for schools, houses of worship tend to have more people congregating in larger areas. This means that the most effective countermeasure may be an armed response. Unlike most public (and even private) schools across the country, houses of worship are typically not bound by state law or school board policy on whether armed personnel can be included as part of the EOP. My recommendation is that as you consider whether an armed staff or armed volunteer program should be included in your house of worship's EOP — and you simply must at least consider it — you follow these steps:

Through a formal or informal poll of your congregation, determine how many of your congregants fall into the following groups:

- Sworn, active-duty law enforcement
- Retired law enforcement eligible to carry a firearm under HR218
- Reserve or other law enforcement
- Active, reserve and retired military
- Civilian firearms instructors
- Llicensed to carry a firearm under your state's concealed carry laws

After understanding the experience and expertise within your congregation, my recommendation is that you form a subcommittee to the EOP planning committee to evaluate the pros and cons of establishing your own armed staff or armed volunteer program. It's my belief that if you've fairly included appropriate expertise on this subcommittee, your list of pros will significantly outweigh your list of cons. In fact, it's likely that your only cons will center around the emotional response to staff members or volunteers carrying firearms rather than any practical objection. Assuming that an armed staff member or armed volunteer program does become part of your plan, you can choose to formalize the program using criteria similar to what I will review in the section on the "Run, Hide, Fight"

methodology. But your discussion of an armed response shouldn't end there.

What Other "Good Guys" Are Already Armed at Your House of Worship?

While there are a number of states that ban the carrying of firearms in houses of worship by statute, the vast majority of states have no such ban. That means individuals licensed to carry a firearm in your state may be legally packing a firearm at the same moment they are taking Holy Communion. Does that alarm you in any way? It shouldn't. The more than 12 million permitholders in the U.S. should be considered among the good guys. They have passed a background check, and the vast majority have received training on the legal and practical aspects of carrying a firearm. So in addition to polling your congregation to find those individuals experienced with firearms, I'd also suggest that you conduct another anonymous poll to find out exactly what percentage of your congregation is already carrying a firearm during services. You might be surprised to find out just how many there are.

While you could end this step after simply conducting the survey, I recommend you hold a separate training course for those individuals so that they understand exactly how they might fit into an overall security plan. Your training for them should include:

- Making them aware that there is a formal program for designated staff members and volunteers to carry a firearm during services or other events. This is an incredibly important step to take to avoid having a well-meaning concealed carry permitholder make an incorrect assumption about who the bad guy is if a mass shooting were to be attempted.
- Include these individuals as part of the team responsible for directing congregants during a lockdown. Those procedures might include directing them to guide congregants to a safe room or through an exterior door. By giving these individuals a formal role, they will be more attuned to the status of a shooter and the status of other armed personnel. This will help in the decision-making process as to whether an evacuation is working or if those congregants should join in on an armed response.
- While concealed-carry permitholders can choose to remain anonymous, having them known to staff

members can avoid the same problem described earlier. It will also lead to more collaboration and a larger feeling of being a team. Either way, it is essential that if, God forbid, there ever is a reason for armed staff or volunteers to draw their sidearms, no one but the attacker gets shot.

Publicly Acknowledging Your Program

In addition to having a "Welcome to our Church/ Temple/Mosque" sign on your front door, I'd also recommend that you include a sign that states "Multiple Armed Personnel on the Premises Will Use Deadly Force to Protect Our Congregation." While some in your congregation might feel that the second sign is counter to your house of worship's mission of peace, you can take comfort in the fact that by creating and publicizing an armed staff member program, you'll very likely never have to use it. Peace and deterrence are two missions that everyone at your house of worship should be able to get behind.

DON'T BE AN EASY VICTIM: RUN, HIDE OR *FIGHT*

AFTER THE MASS SHOOTING IN COLUMBINE, COLORADO, LAW ENFORCEMENT AGENCIES FROM THE FBI DOWN TO LOCAL COUNTIES, CITIES, TOWNS AND VILLAGES got to work on redeveloping agency and interagency operating plans and tactics to address the mass shooter threat from a law enforcement perspective. If we can rewrite the way that law enforcement responds to the threat, we can also rewrite the way that

The changes in operating procedures for law enforcement agencies evolved from the understanding that the mass shooter threat was a very different threat from an armed gunman taking hostages and sharing a list of demands with a negotiator. A different strategy was required to counter the new threat.

One lesson learned from Columbine was that waiting on a SWAT team to arrive before making entry would only ensure more victims would be killed in the intervening minutes. So new tactics evolved which included having the first arriving officer or officers make entry the moment they arrived on the scene of the shooting, even if that meant making entry with just one or two officers. The change in tactic seemed to be a good one. While the Columbine shooting lasted 47 minutes, subsequent mass shootings have averaged a duration of about nine minutes. So tactics for law enforcement evolved, but it wasn't until the federal government's Department of Homeland Security quietly released a program called "Active Shooter: How to Respond" that anyone began to address how *victim* tactics should change. The DHS program, which is better known as, "Run, Hide, Fight," teaches potential victims of mass shootings that they aren't required to simply wait out mass casualty attacks without a plan. Instead, they *must* take an active part in their own self-preservation by either running, hiding or fighting back. While the program doesn't specifically call out this fact, it's important to understand that the "Run, Hide, Fight" methodology doesn't look at those three options linearly, or as a series of steps that you must progress through. If you are in public, at a school, at your house of worship or at your place of business and a mass shooter enters

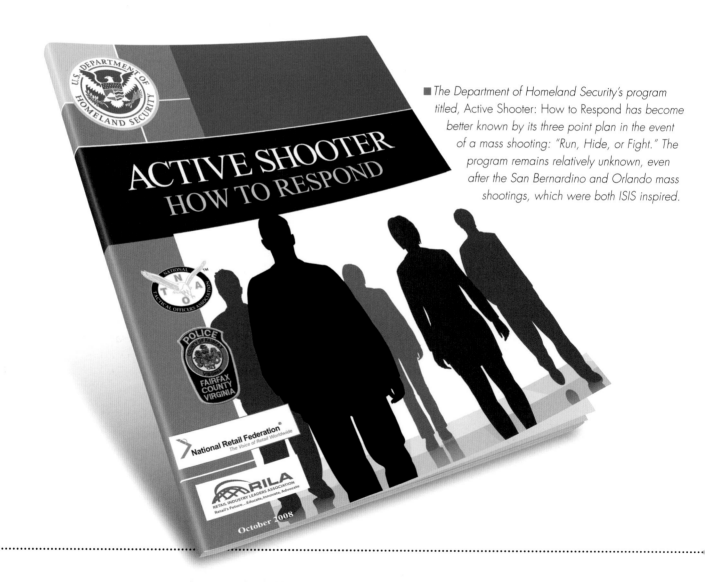

■ *The Department of Homeland Security's program titled, Active Shooter: How to Respond has become better known by its three point plan in the event of a mass shooting: "Run, Hide, or Fight." The program remains relatively unknown, even after the San Bernardino and Orlando mass shootings, which were both ISIS inspired.*

the area, you're not required to first try to run, then hide, before you elect to fight back. If the situation calls for it, you can choose to immediately fight back ... and fight back *aggressively*.

In this section, we'll review "Run, Hide, Fight" in detail where once again I'll supplement the information provided by the DHS with my own recommendations.

DENIAL ISN'T A REQUIRED STEP

Even before we look at specific actions you'll need to take if you elect to run, hide or fight, let's first talk about what your *immediate* reaction must be to the sound of gunfire or other signs that a mass shooter has entered the area. As with many things in life that are out of the ordinary, our first response to a mass shooter threat may be denial. We may think, "This can't be what I think it is." Even momentary denial can lead to the loss of valuable seconds that could have been used to escape or prepare an active counterattack. Whether the first sign of an active shooter is gunfire, the alarm being sounded, lockdown being called, or a text or tweet, you *must* skip the denial step and immediately accept the fact that it is real. You should then try to determine the direction and proximity of the threat. If the alert has not yet been sounded, you must alert others around you by shouting, "Gun, gun, leave the area!" At that point, you'll make a decision as to whether you will run, hide or fight.

Buckeye Alert:
Active Shooter on campus. Run, Hide, Fight. Watts Hall. 19th and College.

■ *At 9:56 a.m. on Nov. 28, 2016, an alert was sent out to all Ohio State students and staff by text and social media, warning them of a possible active shooter on campus and telling them to "Run, Hide, Fight." The problem was that no one knew what "Run, Hide, Fight" meant, since no training had been provided to students or staff.*

If you have the ability and opportunity, your first choice of action should be to run out of the kill zone as fast as you can. Keep running until you've reached what you believe is a safe location. Regardless of whether you're in a wide-open room or a narrow hallway, your No. 1 goal should be to put as much distance between yourself and the shooter as possible. As you exit the area, you must remember that your top priority is your own personal safety. That means leaving all personal belongings behind and even leaving others behind if they are too afraid, unable or unwilling to leave. Head in a direction opposite of the sound of gunfire, then make a direct route for the closest exit.

Even if the shooter enters your immediate area, even the conference room or classroom you're in, escaping may still be an option. But you must *immediately* kick your escape plan into action by running in the opposite direction. Move laterally or diagonally from the shooter to shift off of his line of attack. Anyone who has taken a trip to the range and then tried to translate those static skills to shooting at a moving target while hunting

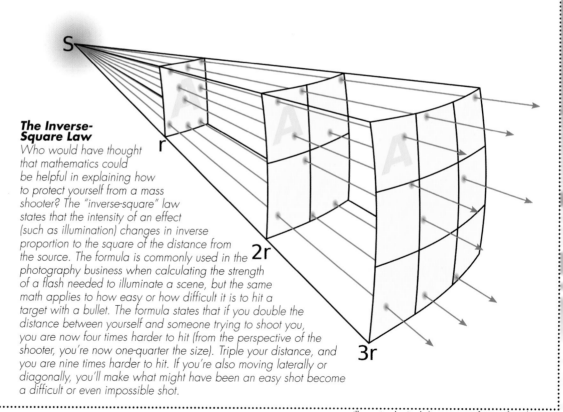

The Inverse-Square Law

Who would have thought that mathematics could be helpful in explaining how to protect yourself from a mass shooter? The "inverse-square" law states that the intensity of an effect (such as illumination) changes in inverse proportion to the square of the distance from the source. The formula is commonly used in the photography business when calculating the strength of a flash needed to illuminate a scene, but the same math applies to how easy or how difficult it is to hit a target with a bullet. The formula states that if you double the distance between yourself and someone trying to shoot you, you are now four times harder to hit (from the perspective of the shooter, you're now one-quarter the size). Triple your distance, and you are nine times harder to hit. If you're also moving laterally or diagonally, you'll make what might have been an easy shot become a difficult or even impossible shot.

Illustration by Borb/Lucasian Professor of Mathematics

can attest to the fact that accurately shooting at a stationary target can be difficult enough. Shooting at a target that is moving laterally or diagonally away from you increases the difficulty exponentially. I actually make that last statement based on mathematical fact, not just as a figure of speech. Back in math class, you might have heard of the "inverse-square law," which states that the intensity of an effect (such as illumination) changes in inverse proportion to the square of the distance from the source. While that description might sound a bit complicated, it means that if you double the distance between an object and a source of light, the intensity of the light on that object isn't one-half of the original intensity. It's one-fourth of the original intensity.

The exact same formula applies to how easy or how difficult it is to hit a target with a firearm. For example, if you are 10 feet from a shooter, simply doubling the distance between you and the shooter makes you four times more difficult to hit. If you triple the distance, you will be nine times more difficult to hit. Increase the distance to 100 feet (which the average person can cover in about 10 seconds), and you've just become 100 times harder to hit (10 times the original distance squared, or $10^2 = 100$). We know that mass shooters will not waste time chasing after victims, especially if those victims are about to leave the immediate area, even more so if other potential victims chose not to run and remain in the area.

HAVE AN ESCAPE PLAN

As simple as running away sounds, having an escape plan first requires you to have a strategy. This can be as simple as always knowing where all room and building exits are. As part of your institution's EOP (or as part of your individual or family plan if no EOP exists), it's important to identify appropriate escape routes in the event of a mass shooting. Similar to knowing escape routes in the event of a fire, there should be at least two identified escape routes from each room. The selection of which escape route to use will be based upon the location and disposition of the shooter. In some cases, exterior doors may be used, while in other cases, exterior windows must be opened or broken to enable a rapid escape. Once clear from the building, you should run as quickly as possible until you've reached law enforcement. Keep your hands in the air and follow the direction of law enforcement personnel to the letter.

Be a Good Witness

If your institution is like most, law enforcement will not have an internal video feed to determine the disposition of the attacker. Officers must either operate in the blind or depend upon eyewitness accounts from those who were able to escape the area. Even if you had just seconds to look at the attacker, try to remember the following key items. They will be critical in helping law enforcement end the attack quickly:

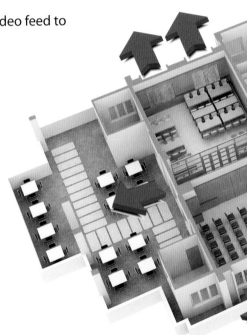

- A general description of the attacker including what he or she is wearing, size, race characteristics, hair color, approximate age, etc.
- A general description of the firearm(s) that the shooter is carrying. For example, is it a handgun, or is it a long gun like a rifle or shotgun?
- Whether the shooter is carrying extra magazines and if so, approximately how many.
- Whether the shooter is carrying a bag or backpack.
- Whether the shooter is wearing body armor, which might be indicated by bulky clothing or a vest.
- The direction of travel of the shooter.
- Anything that the shooter said, such as whether he has a specific target or demands.

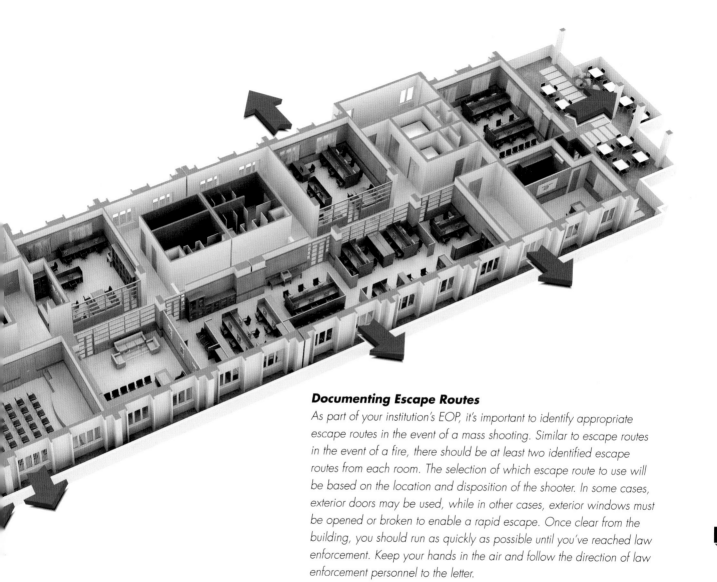

Documenting Escape Routes

As part of your institution's EOP, it's important to identify appropriate escape routes in the event of a mass shooting. Similar to escape routes in the event of a fire, there should be at least two identified escape routes from each room. The selection of which escape route to use will be based on the location and disposition of the shooter. In some cases, exterior doors may be used, while in other cases, exterior windows must be opened or broken to enable a rapid escape. Once clear from the building, you should run as quickly as possible until you've reached law enforcement. Keep your hands in the air and follow the direction of law enforcement personnel to the letter.

If the shooter has not yet seen you and there is no practical escape from the building, you may choose to hide in as safe a place as possible, should one be available and meet the definition of good concealment and cover. Concealment is anything that hides you from the threat (a closed door, wall or anything you can duck behind) while cover also protects you from incoming bullets (concrete pillars, a concrete wall or the front of a vehicle where the engine block is). Concealment may keep you safe, but if the shooter approaches your area, you may be very easy to detect, especially if you are breathing heavily or are with others who are making noise. Cover is a far superior choice since it can not only protect you from incoming bullets, it can also help to keep the noise of you and others down so that you go undetected by the shooter.

If you have chosen to hide, here are key points to remember:

- As part of the EOP your institution developed, you should be aware of which rooms have locks and which rooms do not. Even if you need to travel a greater distance to reach a room with a lock, this will be a far superior choice.
- If you have the choice of hiding in a room on the interior of the building or the exterior of the building, choose the room on the exterior. You may have an opportunity to break a window and escape from the building, or rescuers arriving on the scene may do it for you.
- Once you and others have entered the room, *immediately* lock the door and move out of the line of sight of any windows in or alongside the door. As part of your institution's EOP, the room may have a marked line on the floor indicating the areas inside and outside the line of sight.
- If the room you entered does not have a lock, quickly barricade the door with heavy furniture. Don't be shy about this. If there are tables, chairs and desks in the room, quickly move as much as possible to block the door.
- Turn off the lights.
- Silence all electronic devices.
- Remain silent. Remember that on average, you will only have five to nine minutes to wait until the shooting has ended.
- If possible, use strategies to silently communicate with first responders. For example, in rooms with exterior windows, make signs to silently signal law enforcement and emergency responders to indicate the status of the room's occupants.

- Hide along the wall closest to the exit but out of the view from the hallway (allowing for an ambush of the shooter and for possible escape if the shooter enters the room).
- Find an improvised weapon and have it at the ready in case the shooter forces his way into the room. Silently indicate to others in the room that they should do so as well.
- Remain in place until given an "all-clear" by identifiable law enforcement.

As part of your institution's EOP, it's important to understand which rooms in your school, house of worship or place of business can effectively act as "safe rooms" in the event of an attack. Also, identify those rooms on building schematics placed in each room, no differently than how a fire escape plan is documented. Key criteria for a safe room include:

- A lockable, solid-core door that does not require a key to lock;
- No windows to the interior of the building (other than a viewport on the door);
- An ability to move all occupants of the room out of the line of sight from the viewport; and
- Objects within the room that can serve as barricades and improvised weapons.

Exterior rooms are superior to interior rooms but as long as the interior room meets all other criteria, it is highly likely that occupants can survive the up to nine minutes it will take for the average mass shooting to end. As part of an effective EOP, each safe room should also be pre-staged with an emergency first-aid kit and an intercom or other means of communicating with responders to update them with the status of the room's occupants.

Staging Your Safe Room

As part of your institutional EOP, not only should rooms be identified as safe or not safe, you should also include in the plan the specific items that will be staged in your safe rooms. These items can include:

- An additional ability to block the door, such as a Door Jammer or other commercial device.
- Any required tool to open or break exterior windows if they are an avenue of escape.
- Any required item to block or cover the viewport in the door (if one exists).
- An emergency first-aid kit.
- An ability to communicate with law enforcement. The most sophisticated way to do this would be electronically, such as how Southwestern High has implemented it. A simpler method would be for each safe room to have three pre-printed posters which can be stuck to the exterior windows indicating whether the occupants of the room are "All Safe," "Under Attack," or "Need Medical Assistance."
- A weapon which can be used against the attacker if he makes entry. This can be as well thought out as an expandable baton, as simple as a baseball bat, or as specific as a taser or firearm in a lock box.

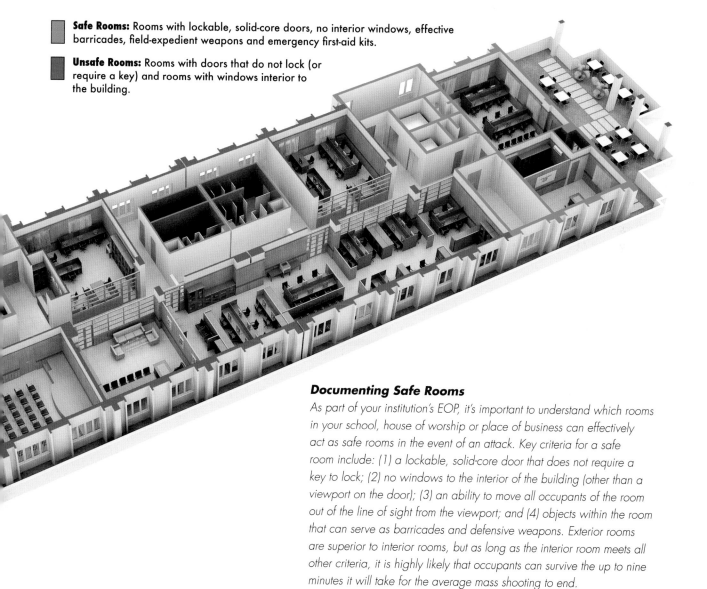

Safe Rooms: Rooms with lockable, solid-core doors, no interior windows, effective barricades, field-expedient weapons and emergency first-aid kits.

Unsafe Rooms: Rooms with doors that do not lock (or require a key) and rooms with windows interior to the building.

Documenting Safe Rooms

As part of your institution's EOP, it's important to understand which rooms in your school, house of worship or place of business can effectively act as safe rooms in the event of an attack. Key criteria for a safe room include: (1) a lockable, solid-core door that does not require a key to lock; (2) no windows to the interior of the building (other than a viewport on the door); (3) an ability to move all occupants of the room out of the line of sight from the viewport; and (4) objects within the room that can serve as barricades and defensive weapons. Exterior rooms are superior to interior rooms, but as long as the interior room meets all other criteria, it is highly likely that occupants can survive the up to nine minutes it will take for the average mass shooting to end.

As part of an effective EOP, each safe room should also be pre-staged with a first-aid kit and an intercom or other means of communicating with responders about the status of the room's occupants.

FIGHT

If it's too late to run or the shooter finds your hiding spot and escape is not possible, you have just a single choice remaining. At that point, you must commit to aggressive action to stop the shooter, and you must use whatever means necessary. That may mean using improvised weapons that you find on the scene, or it may mean using a firearm if you had the foresight to include one in your personal or institutional plan.

While the "Run, Hide, Fight" program doesn't specifically take a stance one way or another on whether a firearm in the hands of potential victims would change the outcome, it is significant that the DHS recommends fighting back at all. I'll add that the European version of this program is "Run, Hide, *Report*."

Had "Run, Hide, Fight" been taught to the students at Virginia Tech, it's likely that even if the shooter hadn't been incapacitated by his potential victims, any aggressive action on the part of the students would have disrupted hiss momentum and his confidence, forcing him to move from offensive mode to defensive mode. Remember that mass shooters count on being entirely in control of the situation. A coordinated response by the students to fight back would have threatened that control. As discussed in Part One, the students in classrooms 204, 206, 207 and 211 didn't necessarily need to incapacitate or kill the attacker. All they needed to do was buy themselves several minutes of time to allow law enforcement to make entry (as the students in classroom 205 did). Remember that the average length of time that mass shooting events last is only nine minutes, or in the Virginia Tech case, 11 minutes, since he had chained and padlocked several doors. What could the students have done to hold out for 11 minutes? As soon as it was apparent that a shooter was in the building, the students could have immediately piled tables, chairs, bookshelves or any other barrier objects in front of the door. Each student could have then picked up a chair, a book, a coffee mug, shoes or any of the hundreds of other objects that would have been in the classroom. If the murderer were able to breach the barriers and enter the classroom, the students could have thrown those objects at his head and torso, screaming at the top of their lungs, *committing* to their actions. If he went down still in possession of his firearms, the students could then have beaten him into unconsciousness with chairs, fists or feet. If that sounds pretty brutal, the alternative was more so — the murder of 30 innocent people in Norris Hall.

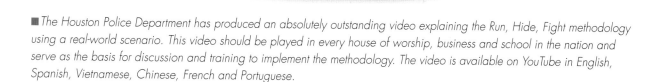

■ *The Houston Police Department has produced an absolutely outstanding video explaining the Run, Hide, Fight methodology using a real-world scenario. This video should be played in every house of worship, business and school in the nation and serve as the basis for discussion and training to implement the methodology. The video is available on YouTube in English, Spanish, Vietnamese, Chinese, French and Portuguese.*

IMPROVISED WEAPONS

We'll talk about how firearms may fit into your personal or institutional plan in a moment, but let's talk about improvised weapons first. As would have been the case in the classrooms in Norris Hall at Virginia Tech, we're typically surrounded by dozens of objects, large and small, which could be used as improvised weapons to disable or deflect an attacker. While any object thrown at an attacker's head will cause him to temporarily break off his attack as he turns to dodge, your first choice should be any hardened object that can be used as an impact weapon, such as a chair, the leg from a table, a lamppost or a laptop. Also use any object that can serve as an improvised edged weapon, such as a scissors or a utility knife. Other objects, including shoes, coffee mugs, books or even papers thrown at the attacker's head will cause at least an involuntary reaction to turn away from the improvised missiles, which can allow other defenders to reach the attacker and overwhelm him.

To improve the likelihood of success, I'll echo what the DHS has to say about fighting back: You must commit to your actions until the shooter is overwhelmed and either disabled or dead. If you're unsure of how easy it will be to find an improvised weapon, the next time you're at your child's school, your house of worship, your place of business or even out in public shopping, take a critical look around at the objects in the room in which you find yourself. You can even make a game of it to drive some creative thinking on how you can take an everyday object and turn it into a weapon. To give this a try, look at the photo on the opposite page of a typical office and try to identify as many improvised weapons as you can. When you've completed your list, flip the page to compare your list to mine.

Counterattacking as a Team

While the chances of a single defender overwhelming an attacker with an improvised weapon might seem low, if multiple defenders counterattack as a team, attacking the shooter simultaneously from multiple directions, the likelihood of success will be dramatically increased. Logic might state that the best time for a counterattack is when the shooter is reloading (remember that the Virginia Tech shooter reloaded a total of 15 times) but waiting for a reload may simply mean delaying the counterattack while more victims are shot. Since action always beats reaction, defenders rushing in from multiple directions will have, on average, about 1.5 seconds before the shooter can react to their actions. During that 1.5 seconds, the defenders can close the gap by 20 to 25 feet. Considering that no mass shooter has ever exceeded firing two rounds per second, the mathematics work in favor of the defenders.

These types of improvised weapons are clearly weapons of last resort. If your opportunity to escape or to hide has disappeared, and your options are to either plead with the shooter to spare your life or to fight back to your last breath, you *must fight back* with whatever you can. You must be willing to get as brutal and as bloody as is required to stop the shooter, even if that means clubbing him to death with the metal

■ *How many improvised weapons can you find in the photo above? Search for both disabling weapons (weapons which can kill or disable the attacker) and distracting weapons (objects thrown at the attacker, causing him to flinch and providing valuable time for a counterattack, especially if that counterattack is coming from multiple directions and multiple defenders all working as a team). Flip the page to compare your list of improvised weapons against mine.*

leg of an office table. Remember that in 23 of the 165 active shooting events tracked by the FBI, bystanders were successfully able to subdue the shooter and end the attack with nothing more than fists or improvised weapons that they found on-scene. These shooters can be beat. But if you'd like to dramatically improve your odds of success, you'll need to include an armed response in your personal or institutional plan.

AN ARMED RESPONSE

For 12 million Americans, carrying a firearm on a daily basis with a state-issued concealed-carry permit is as everyday as carrying a wallet or purse. But for most school boards, church committees and corporate lawyers, the thought of including firearms in an EOP may be a difficult idea to swallow. If you fall into that camp, my suggestion is that you play this scenario through in your mind: 30 seconds from now, a mass shooter will walk into the front door of your school, house of worship or business. He will shoot and kill the first three people he sees, just feet away from you. You and a dozen others have no chance to run or hide. In this scenario, you get to pick three extra people to join you. Those people could be friends who will call the police, though you know that the shooting will last about nine more minutes before the shooter kills himself or the police stop him. You can choose three psychologists or spiritual leaders who will plead with the shooter not to kill anyone else and to give himself up, but you know that only 4 percent of active shooters surrender. You can choose three friends who have taken karate classes, or you can choose to have three friends join you who are legally armed.

While you may consider this scenario overly dramatic, I use it to illustrate the fact that just because these evildoers are using firearms as an *offensive* tool does not mean that you should be dissuaded from considering a firearm as a *defensive* tool. The truth of the matter is that nothing else in the world can level the playing field between a demented murderer and a senior citizen, expectant mother or a disabled veteran. Nothing. If you ever do find yourself face to face with a mass shooter, having a gun in your possession won't guarantee that you'll survive, but *not* having one increases the odds that you, and everyone standing behind you, will be dead.

Does an Armed Response Belong in Your EOP?

If the idea of creating an armed educator, employee or volunteer program made up of non-law enforcement officers sounds revolutionary, it isn't. Since Sandy Hook, hundreds of houses of worship and school districts, and thousands of businesses both public and private, have done exactly that. While these institutions can choose to require nothing more than a state-issued concealed carry permit for participants in armed staff programs, many are requiring additional training and qualifications as part of a formal EOP. Those additional requirements often include:

- Participants attend weapons retention and advanced handgun training. This training is often modeled after the armed pilot program started after 9/11, but typically does not require more than two weeks. This training usually includes advanced weapons handling; weapon retention; legal topics, such as the use of deadly force; and multiple shoot/no-shoot scenarios in a variety of settings using live fire and Simunition firearms and ammunition.
- Participants pass a physical agility test and/or a psychological test to enter an armed staff program, similar to the type of tests required during the application process for a police, EMS or firefighter position.
- Firearms be secured in what are referred to as *Level III retention holsters*. Level III holsters have three active retention methods which keep the firearm locked into the holster until the retention methods are properly released, all in the correct order. When the

Did you find these improvised weapons? What others did you find?

1 ■ Roller Chair
The roller chair can be picked up and swung at or thrown at an attacker, or the bottom can be unscrewed and used as an impact weapon.

2 ■ Computer Monitor or Laptop
The computer monitor (or the typical laptop found in most offices) can also be used as an impact weapon.

3 ■ Desktop Speaker
The desktop speaker can be thrown or swung at the end of its cord as an improvised mace.

4 ■ Scissors
The scissors can be used as improvised edged weapons. Since scissors will have more difficulty penetrating the chest or abdominal wall when compared to a knife, focus on stabbing the attacker in and around the face and neck.

5 ■ Pens and Pencils
While not as effective as other improvised edged weapons, stabbing an attacker in and around the face and neck with a pen or pencil can allow other defenders to subdue him.

6 ■ Table Legs
Perhaps the best improvised weapons in the room are the legs of the table, which can be quickly broken off if enough force is applied. If multiple defenders simultaneously attacked a shooter from multiple directions with these improvised striking weapons, the shooter could be quickly disabled or killed.

7 ■ Computer Cords
While one or more defenders counterattack a shooter with other improvised weapons, another defender could use a computer cord as a make-shift garrote to kill him, or at least cause him to lose consciousness.

8 ■ Folding Chairs
Five folding chairs in this room equal five improvised weapons for defenders. If just one defender attacks a shooter with a folding chair, he or she would most likely be shot. But if five defenders attack a shooter simultaneously from multiple directions, the shooter would most likely be stopped in place.

9 ■ Distracting Weapons
In addition to the improvised disabling weapons, the room is literally filled with other objects that can be thrown at an attacker's head to distract him or cause a momentary flinch, allowing other defenders to close with him. Papers, books and boxes on the shelves, the paperweight on the desk and even the potted plants on the upper right shelf could serve as ad-hoc missiles. Don't forget about shoes, coffee mugs or belts and, of course, your fists, elbows and feet.

firearm operator has also been trained in weapons retention, an unauthorized person has virtually no chance of gaining access to the firearm.

Some Comments on the Use of Deadly Force

Prior to applying for a concealed carry permit, most states require that the applicant attend an appropriate training course, which usually includes a healthy dose of what the law has to say about when deadly force may be used against an assailant. Most instructors also provide students with a variety of real-life scenarios, including hypothetical robberies, carjackings and other threats of assault. In some cases, the "right" answer for a scenario might be that deadly force would be authorized, while other scenarios are meant to show that the threshold for the use of deadly force may not have been met and should not be used. Because the rules governing the use of deadly force can often sound complex, students can leave their concealed carry class worrying that they'll either hesitate too long when deadly force is required and they'll end up dead, or that they'll use deadly force when it wasn't legally authorized and end up in jail. Let's clear up those concerns in the context of a mass shooting, because if you have the opportunity to stop a shooter with deadly force and you hesitate, not only will you die, but others around you will most likely die as well. To state it as clearly as possible: If a mass shooter has entered your immediate area and is firing on bystanders, the legal threshold for the use of deadly force *has been met*. If you make the decision to engage the shooter, it's very important to understand that you must *commit to your response*. Do not hesitate, attempt to fire a disabling shot or give the shooter a verbal warning. Let me say that last part again — when returning fire, you have no legal or moral obligation to verbally challenge the mass shooter, such as telling him, "Stop or I'll shoot!" Doing so would only give the shooter the opportunity to shoot at you first. I'll go as far as saying that your moral obligation would be to return fire as quickly as possible with no hesitation, giving the shooter no warning at all, even if that means putting multiple rounds into his back.

Additionally, attempting to fire a disabling shot, such as trying to shoot the attacker's firing hand, is a skill that should be left to Hollywood action heroes. It's a cold reality, but the fastest, surest, safest way (for innocent bystanders, not safest to the attacker) to end the attack is to use the method taught to every police agency in the U.S.: aim for the attacker's "cardiovascular triangle." When the cardiovascular triangle isn't visible, police are taught to shoot at the "center of exposed mass," which is the center of the largest part of the attacker's body that's visible. If shots to the cardiovascular triangle do not stop the shooter (if, for example, he is wearing body armor), my suggestion would be to march your shots lower in an attempt to hit the pelvic girdle before attempting a head shot. Striking the pelvic girdle will bring even the most determined attacker to the floor, which may allow any bystanders remaining in the area the opportunity to escape.

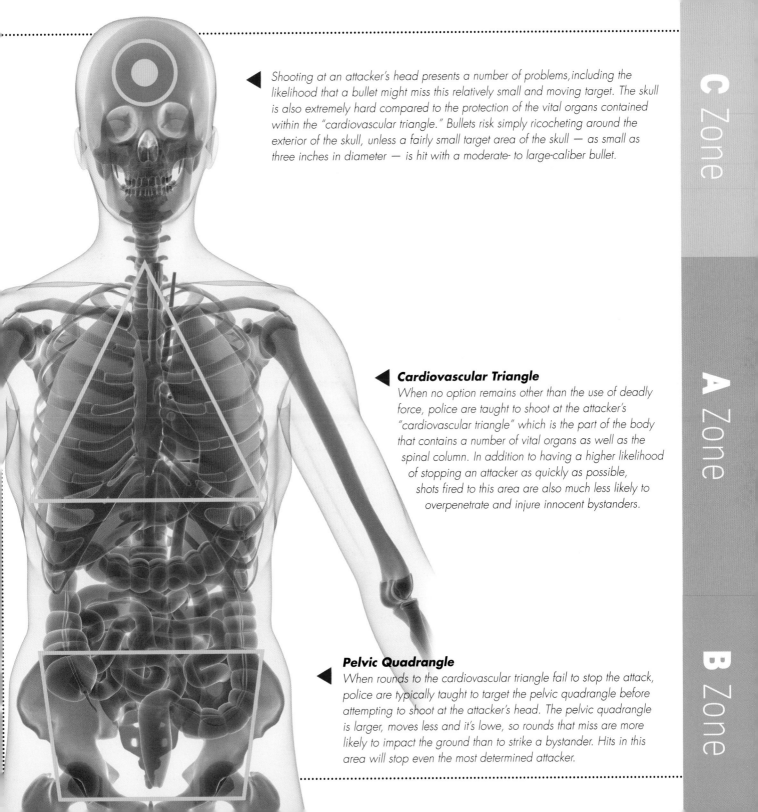

Shooting at an attacker's head presents a number of problems, including the likelihood that a bullet might miss this relatively small and moving target. The skull is also extremely hard compared to the protection of the vital organs contained within the "cardiovascular triangle." Bullets risk simply ricocheting around the exterior of the skull, unless a fairly small target area of the skull — as small as three inches in diameter — is hit with a moderate- to large-caliber bullet.

Cardiovascular Triangle

When no option remains other than the use of deadly force, police are taught to shoot at the attacker's "cardiovascular triangle" which is the part of the body that contains a number of vital organs as well as the spinal column. In addition to having a higher likelihood of stopping an attacker as quickly as possible, shots fired to this area are also much less likely to overpenetrate and injure innocent bystanders.

Pelvic Quadrangle

When rounds to the cardiovascular triangle fail to stop the attack, police are typically taught to target the pelvic quadrangle before attempting to shoot at the attacker's head. The pelvic quadrangle is larger, moves less and it's lowe, so rounds that miss are more likely to impact the ground than to strike a bystander. Hits in this area will stop even the most determined attacker.

C Zone

A Zone

B Zone

Are Traditional Firearms the Only Option?

In addition to including traditional firearms and ammunition in any armed staff program, I'd also suggest Simunition firearms and ammunition be considered. Since the late 1980s, law enforcement agencies have trained with Simunition firearms and ammo, which use modified firearms along with ammunition containing a hard plastic bullet and a low propellant charge rather than a lead or copper bullet and a full charge. This allows officers the ability to train in realistic, force-on-force scenarios and to fire on mock attackers. Although Simunition rounds are plastic rather than lead or copper, they do carry a solid punch. These rounds will typically cause the mock attacker to break off his attack rather than fighting his or her way through the pain. Used as a defensive tool, Simunition firearms stand a good chance of driving a mass shooter out of the immediate area or temporarily incapacitating him. While Simunition firearms and ammunition can't achieve the same stopping power as traditional firearms, I believe that including a Simunition option would have the side benefit of attracting more people to join an armed staff program. If your institution has the choice of ending up with just two staff members who are trained and authorized to carry traditional firearms or those two staff members plus eight more authorized to carry Simunition sidearms, your institution will be a safer place. The fact is, mass shooters are unlikely to know the difference between the sound or the pain inflicted by Simunition rounds and live rounds. (If you've ever been hit by a Simunition round, you know what I mean.) We also need to keep in mind that the moment they believe a counterattack is occurring, rapid mass murderers end the attack or their own life.

I also believe there may be another significant benefit of allowing staff members to choose a Simunition firearm over a traditional firearm. Knowing that they'll only inflict pain rather than death on the shooter or innocent bystanders, staff members may be much more likely to immediately commit to a response rather than hesitating as they might with a traditional firearm and ammunition. Picture what might have changed at Sandy Hook if Principal Dawn Hochsprung and School Psychologist Mary Sherlach had closed in on the shooter, firing Simunition rounds at his head and torso as fast as their sidearms' triggers could be pressed, instead of simply shouting, "Stay put!" as Principal Hochsprung was reported to have done. The attacker would either have

■ *Simunition utilizes a low propellant charge and plastic bullets along with modified firearms, which allow law enforcement officers and military personnel to train in realistic force-on-force scenarios. This way, defenders are able to fire upon mock attackers. Although the plastic bullets are non-lethal, they do pack a significant punch, requiring that trainees wear protective eyewear and other gear to avoid ending training covered in bruises or blinded. Although designed for training, Simunition firearms and ammunition shouldn't be discounted as a defensive tool to use against a potential mass shooter.*

ended his life immediately or collapsed into the fetal position as his body was wracked with painful impact after painful impact. Even if he had recovered his senses long enough to continue his attack, the disruption of his momentum would certainly have bought the teachers in classrooms 8 and 10 enough time to lock the doors, and it could have bought the police the few minutes needed to make entry and end the attack.

Making a Case for Armed Educators

While the thought of arming staff members at a house of worship may be a difficult idea to swallow for many parishioners, the thought of creating an armed educator program has traditionally met with even more resistance. The typical argument against arming educators is that teachers are trained to teach, not to carry a firearm. But a similar argument was used against arming pilots before the hugely successful armed pilot program was created. The truth is, pilots and educators have several things in common. Teachers and pilots are highly intelligent people; if they can learn how to fly an aircraft or explain the Magna Carta, then they can learn how to handle a firearm. Both groups come highly vetted, with some teachers even having passed both background and psychological tests as pilots do. And both groups' job descriptions includes protecting those people who fall under their direct care. School districts in the states of Arkansas, Colorado, Idaho, Kansas, Mississippi, Ohio, Oregon, Texas, Utah and Wisconsin now have formalized armed educator programs written into state law and passed in the aftermath of Sandy Hook. Texas is one of the leaders in the movement, with more than 100

school districts now having fully staffed and trained participants. As of August 2016, even California has joined the movement, adding five armed and trained teachers at a high school in Fresno. To understand the difference that these on-scene, armed educators might make, see the graphic on the following page which starkly lays out the number of teachers and students that will die during each stage of a typical school attack. Ending an attack early *will* save lives.

If you're wondering why all schools haven't implemented a program like this, it's because the gun-control forces in this country want you and members of school boards to believe that a physically fit teacher wearing a Level III holster, trained in weapon-retention and who has successfully completed multiple live-fire scenarios, is more dangerous to your children than a school shooter who walks through the front door loaded with multiple firearms and hundreds of rounds of ammunition. It's time that you politely but vocally disagree with that opinion. School boards may also argue that there is a need to balance security and access, or that armed teachers or staff members will "scare the children." That fact is, those arguments are bunk. No one makes the "access versus security" argument about airplane cockpits or the secure area of airports. Children also know the difference between a good guy with a gun and a bad guy with a gun. Good guys with guns provide a sense of comfort and security, not fear. Ask yourself this: How safe would you or your children feel if the extent of airport security were "No Guns Allowed" signs posted at every entrance and cockpits had glass doors? The fact is, an armed educator program at any

The Case for Arming Teachers

To understand just how many lives could be saved if armed educators ended an attack early, the chart below shows how long stages of the average school shooting last and how many victims died during each, averaged from the five worst school shootings.

AVERAGE TIME DELAY BEFORE VICTIMS CALL 911

2 MINUTES

AVERAGE TIME FOR A 911 DISPATCHER TO RECEIVE A CALL, TRANSFER THAT DATA TO AN OUTBOUND DISPATCHER, AND FOR THAT DISPATCHER TO ALERT UNITS

30 SECONDS

AVERAGE TIME FOR POLICE UNITS TO ARRIVE ON THE SCENE OF A MASS SHOOTING AFTER BEING DISPATCHED

4 MINUTES

AVERAGE TIME FOR POLICE TO MAKE ENTRY AFTER ARRIVING ON SCENE

3 MINUTES

given school would most likely guarantee that the school would never be the subject of an attack. What's more likely to stop a shooter: A "No Guns Allowed" sign taped to a glass door, or a sign declaring, "Armed Personnel on the Premises Will Use Deadly Force to Protect Our Students and Staff" taped to a reinforced steel door?

When a would-be shooter realizes that he will have neither the time nor the opportunity required for his rampage, it's not like he'll decide it's time to go super high-tech and try to beat all of the security measures. He'll go elsewhere.

As you're developing your EOP, don't forget the value of *deterrence*.

WHICH SIGN OFFERS A BETTER DETERRENT TO THE POTENTIAL MASS SHOOTER?

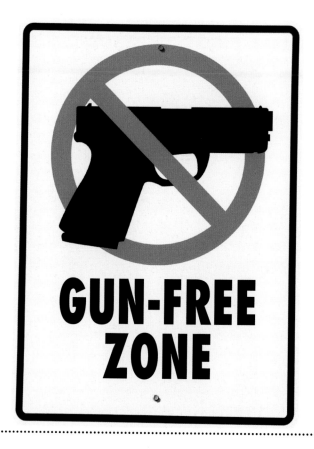

GUN-FREE ZONE

STAFF HEAVILY ARMED AND TRAINED

ANY ATTEMPT TO HARM CHILDREN WILL BE MET WITH <u>DEADLY</u> <u>FORCE</u>

TRIAGE AND TREAT THE WOUNDED

AFTER EVERY MASS SHOOTING, WE'RE INUNDATED WITH NUMBERS. The number of rounds fired. The number of minutes the event lasted. The number of dead and the number of wounded. But a number that I've always wondered about, is how many of the dead could have been saved if triage and treatment had been started by bystanders prior to the entry of EMS professionals — even before the mass shooting ended?

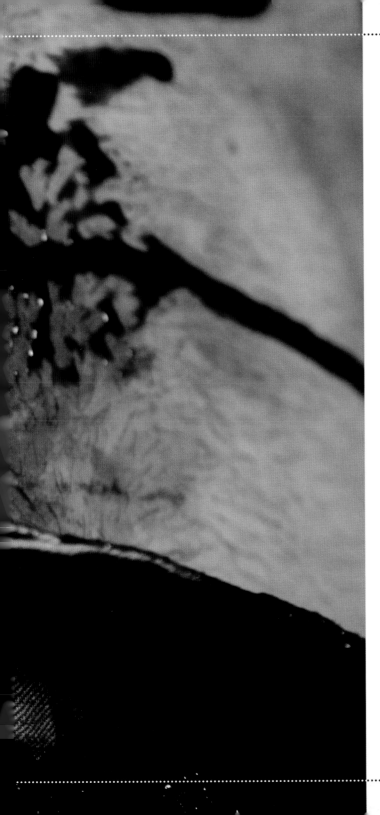

What comes to mind when you hear the phrase, "Mass Casualty Incident?" For most people, the phrase might evoke an image of massive carnage caused by a natural disaster, a fire, a major traffic accident or a train derailment. Or the phrase might evoke the image of the bloody aftermath of a mass shooting.

But a Mass Casualty Incident, or MCI, actually has a very simple definition: It's any event where the number of victims needing immediate care is greater than the number of rescuers immediately available. As an example, if an EMS crew of two arrives on the scene of a traffic accident and there are three victims needing immediate care, then that incident would be categorized as an MCI by the crew. EMS personnel would need to follow a different set of procedures than if there were just a single patient needing care. The fact that they are outnumbered by patients means that the professionals will be unable to provide every patient with immediate care, even those who have significant life threats. When the MCI is a mass shooting, the problem will be compounded because law enforcement on the scene will delay the entry of EMS until the scene has been declared secure. That means that law enforcement must first confirm that any murderers are dead or in custody and that there are no further threats to rescuers, specifically improvised explosive devices. Though many of those in law enforcement are cross-trained as EMTs or paramedics, they are trained to bypass even critically injured victims when first entering the scene of a mass shooting. Instead, the one and only priority will be to neutralize the threat. No priority will be higher for them. Even if they could stop and tend to the wounded, law enforcement officers will be unlikely to carry more than a tourniquet or an emergency bandage on them. It might be critical

minutes before EMS personnel with a higher level of training and more elaborate equipment are on-scene and cleared for entry. That means that it may be up to uninjured bystanders to protect the life of critically injured victims until that patient's care can be handed off to a professional rescuer. If you found yourself in that situation, would you know where to start?

If the answer is no, you can learn to use the same procedure that the professionals will use, which is to immediately triage the victims in your immediate area and then begin the process of providing life-sustaining

The Clock Is Ticking...

Severe bleeding or a penetration to the chest from a gunshot wound must be treated and corrected within four to five minutes, or the patient risks almost certain death. Keep in mind that the average mass shooting lasts nine minutes and it will be even longer before EMS personnel are cleared to make entry.

In the aftermath of a mass shooting, whether a victim lives or dies may be more dependent upon the treatment provided by other, less critically injured victims rather than what the professional rescuers do when they arrive on the scene minutes later.

care. The term "triage" shouldn't be something that frightens you or leads you to believe that you'll need to rise to the skill level of an emergency room surgeon. Instead, it simply gives you an orderly set of steps to follow to determine which victims can wait, which need immediate care and which patients have needs that are beyond the capabilities of lay rescuers.

IMPLEMENTING TRIAGE

When you look at the word *triage*, don't let the prefix fool you. Modern applications of triage actually separate patients into *four* groups rather than three. The French get to take credit, not only for the name (derived from the French word *trier*, which means to "separate out") but also for the creation of the triage system itself. It was first used during the Napoleonic Wars and then refined by French surgeons on the battlefields of World War I. Today, in most modern EMS protocols when a triage has been activated, patients will be separated into the following groups, listed in priority order from lowest to highest:

MINOR

1. **MINOR (Green):** This category will include victims who may be injured but do not have immediate life threats. These patients are often referred to as the "walking wounded." In fact, the simplest way to separate these patients from other more seriously injured victims is to request in a loud, command voice that all victims who can walk, move to a separate area. That area might be on one side of the room, another room entirely or an identified location outside. This initial separation does not mean that those individuals will receive no care at all. It simply means that if they still have adequate strength to move themselves, they can wait for care until victims with more urgent, life-threatening injuries are cared for.

DELAYED

2. **DELAYED (Yellow):** This category includes all patients who are not able to walk on their own but pass all other criteria on the Triage Checklist on pages 158 and 159. These patients may have serious but non-life threatening injuries. However, care may need to be delayed five minutes or more while other patients with a significant life threat, such as severe bleeding or an open chest wound, are cared for and stabilized.

IMMEDIATE

3. **IMMEDIATE (Red):** Patients in this category have immediate life threats which may still be mitigated, even considering the limited resources and equipment. In other words, these patients stand a good chance of being saved.

BEYOND CURRENT CARE

4. BEYOND CURRENT CARE (Black): Patients in this category are either confirmed dead or they have failed all of the criteria on the Triage Checklist. For a patient you believe is not clinically dead (for example, they may not be breathing but may still have a weak heartbeat), it will be an incredibly difficult choice to place them into this category. You must consider the alternative. If you delay treatment to a patient who falls into the Immediate category in an attempt to save a patient who falls into the Beyond Current Care category, the result may be two dead patients rather than one. I'll add that in a traditional triage system, this category is usually referred to as Deceased, even if the patient isn't yet clinically dead. For our purposes, I've renamed this

category Beyond Current Care, which simply means that the needs are beyond the capabilities of the immediate rescuers on scene.

5. It is very important that you understand the following: If you've chosen to place a victim into this category, you have not consigned that person to death. Professional rescuers may be just minutes or seconds away. Instead, you may have changed the outcome of another patient who would have died if you had delayed treatment.

Triage Tags

While it might seem defeatist to include formal triage cards in your emergency supplies stored in safe rooms, the reality is that conducting a triage and tagging patients even prior to EMS arrival can save lives. Even if you've done nothing more than separated the "walking wounded" from the more seriously injured, you'll have cut down on the delay that will occur between the arrival of EMS on scene and the life-saving treatment that they'll provide.

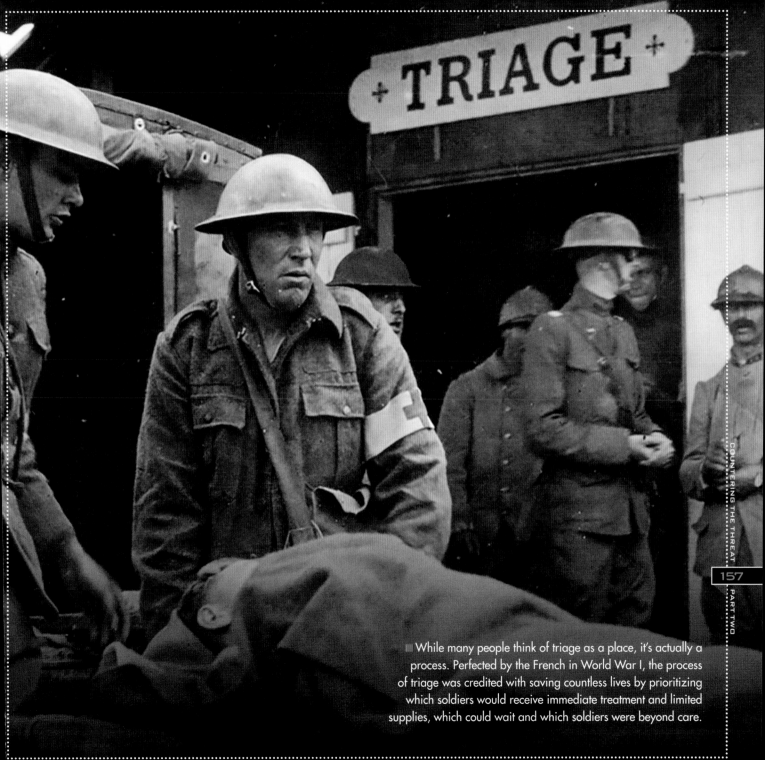

TRIAGE

While many people think of triage as a place, it's actually a process. Perfected by the French in World War I, the process of triage was credited with saving countless lives by prioritizing which soldiers would receive immediate treatment and limited supplies, which could wait and which soldiers were beyond care.

Can the Patient Walk?

The simplest way to separate the walking wounded from the rest is to ask in a command voice that all victims who are able, move to a designated area. All other patients will then be evaluated.

YES →

MINOR

NO

Is the Patient Breathing?

If the patient is talking, you can conclude that his or her airway is open and that he or she is breathing. If your patient is unconscious or has an altered level of consciousness, you'll need to "look, listen and feel" by placing your ear to the patient's mouth, watching for the chest to rise, listening for breathing and feeling for his or her breath on your ear. If your patient is not breathing, you will make ONE attempt to open the airway before moving on to other patients whose lives may still be saved.

YES

Is the Radial Pulse Present?

To check for a radial pulse, apply pressure with the fingertips of your index and middle finger directly on top of the hard tendons beneath the wrist, then slide those fingers into the indentation next to those tendons.

NO

Is the Patient Breathing After Opening the Airway?

For patients that are not breathing, one attempt should be made to restart spontaneous breathing by performing the head-tilt/chin-lift procedure. This is done by pressing down on the patient's forehead and lifting the chin, which typically clears the tongue from the airway. In a non-mass casualty situation, the next step would be to deliver rescue breaths if the patient did not begin spontaneously breathing on his or her own. However, during an MCI, if the patient does not begin breathing on his or her own after opening the airway, you MUST move on to another patient whose life may still be saved with the appropriate treatment.

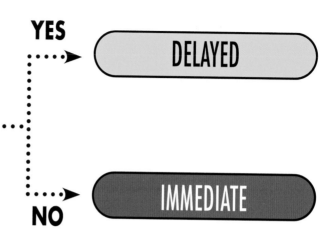

YES ·····▶ DELAYED

Does the Patient Follow Simple Commands?
If the patient is able to follow your simple commands and is oriented to time, place and events, you may delay his or her treatment until other, more critically injured patients are dealt with. If the patient cannot follow simple commands, this may be a sign of severe shock or head trauma.

YES ·····▶

·····▶ IMMEDIATE
NO

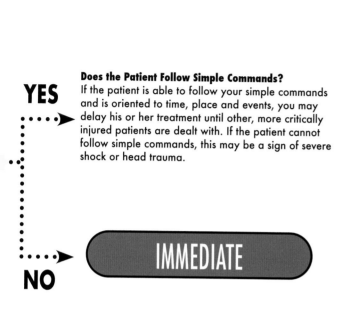

YES ·····▶

·····▶ IMMEDIATE
NO

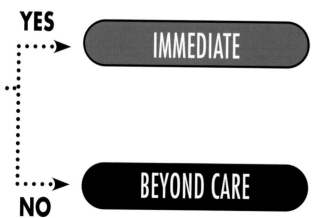

YES ·····▶ IMMEDIATE

·····▶ BEYOND CARE
NO

IMMEDIATE LIFE THREATS

In the aftermath of a mass shooting incident, your focus must be on treating immediate life threats of patients falling into the Immediate category. Immediate life threats from gunshot injuries can include:

- Serious arterial bleeding characterized by bright red, spurting blood
- A penetrating chest wound, known as an open pneumothorax or a "sucking chest wound"
- A gunshot injury to the abdominal cavity
- In addition to the underlying injury itself, your patient may also be suffering from a life-threatening condition known as shock

While the emergency care for each of these life threats has a field-expedient option, my recommendation is to include the creation or purchase of emergency first-aid kits as part of your EOP. Pre-stage them in all rooms that you have designated as safe rooms. My suggestion would be to include the following items at a minimum:

- Two SOFTT or CAT tourniquets
- Three or more compression bandages such as an Emergency/Israeli bandage or H-Bandage
- Two hemostatic dressings
- Five surgical sponges
- Two or more vented chest seals, such as the Bolin Chest Seal (BCS)
- Two large trauma dressings
- An occlusive barrier (a sterile sheet of plastic)
- A blanket
- Triage tags

In the next several sections, we'll review the use of each of these products.

Treating Severe Arterial Bleeding

Severe arterial bleeding is characterized by blood that is spurting, blood that has a "pulse" (meaning when the heart beats, the blood spurts) or blood that is bright red as a result of being highly oxygenated. While less-serious bleeding should still be cared for, serious arterial bleeding can end a patient's life in minutes. Because of this, it's going to take precedence over any other trauma uncovered during a rapid trauma assessment.

Direct Pressure

Even prior to selecting a more aggressive intervention, the rescuer should immediately provide direct, significant pressure to the injury. Direct pressure can be applied with nothing more than a gloved hand, a clean cloth like a shirt or towel, or a stack of sterile gauze or surgical sponges. This immediate, direct pressure is critical even if another individual is preparing a more advanced intervention, such as a tourniquet. Once pressure has been applied, do not remove the cloth, gauze or sponge to check the injury. If the gauze or sponge become soaked in blood, simply layer more gauze or another sponge on top and continue the direct pressure.

Hemostatic Dressings

Serious bleeding can also be controlled by using a hemostatic dressing such as a QuikClot or Celox sponge. While not cheap, hemostatic dressings are impregnated with a compound that absorbs the fluid in blood, leading to more rapid clotting than with a surgical sponge or gauze alone. If you have immediate access to a hemostatic dressing, it should be placed directly on top of or packed into the wound with direct pressure applied for two to three minutes, which allows the clotting action to take effect. Once the bleeding has been controlled, a compression bandage can be placed next, holding the hemostatic dressing in place and applying additional pressure. Hemostatic solutions from QuikClot and Celox include sponges, z-folded gauze which is valuable if a deep penetrating wound must be packed tightly to control the bleeding and as granules that can be poured directly into the wound. Celox has even developed a solution called the *Celox-A Applicator*, which is a pre-packed, large-bore syringe containing 6 grams of Celox granules. This solution allows the hemostatic granules to be injected deep into a penetrating injury, allowing the granules to reach the source of the bleeding. As with all trauma and first-aid gear, possible users should receive professional training in its use.

Celox-A Applicator
Using an innovative method of injecting hemostatic granules deep into a gunshot wound, the Celox-A Applicator can stop severe bleeding when direct pressure or wound packing may fail. The Celox-A Applicator would be appropriate for deep gunshot injuries in the extremities, as well as groin, shoulder or armpit areas, but should not be used for penetrating injuries to the chest or abdominal cavities.

Compression Bandages

Units like the Emergency Bandage (or "Israeli Bandage" as it's often called) or the H-Bandage shown below are appropriate solutions for gunshot injuries to the extremities, the abdomen or the head. Compression bandages are simple in design. Through the use of an elasticized wrapping and a plastic pressure plate, they are able to apply many times the pressure that could be applied by traditional gauze wrapping alone. While there are many commercially available compression bandages, my personal preference is for the H-Bandage. It is an easy-to-use, highly elasticized bandage and the addition of Velcro "brakes" every 12 inches prevents the spool from unrolling if it's accidentally dropped while being applied.

To effectively use a compression bandage to stop severe bleeding, it's critical to wrap the bandage good and tight with each revolution. While your patient might complain that you're wrapping it too tight, the alternative may be that his ot her artery continues to bleed uncontrolled. For a step-by-step explanation of how to apply the H-Bandage, see the opposite page.

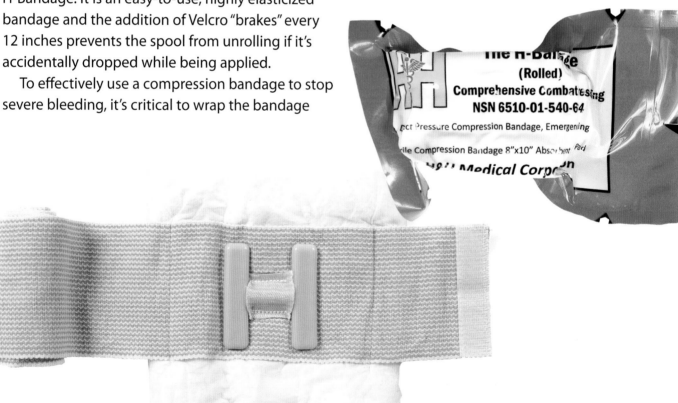

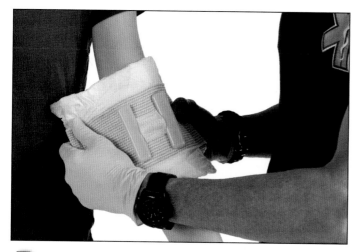

Step 1: Remove the H-Bandage from its outer packaging. Open it up and place the thick, sterile pad directly over the injury.

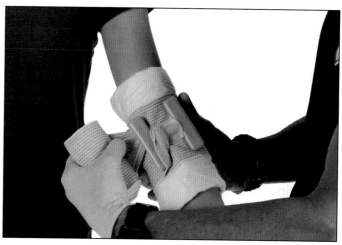

Step 2: Pull tightly to stretch the elastic and wrap the bandage around the limb once. A Velcro tab on the back of the bandage will hold it in place while you position it. Loop the elastic wrap around one side of the "H" then pull tightly and reverse direction.

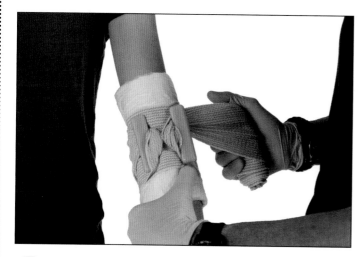

Step 3: Loop the bandage around the other side of the "H." Reverse direction again and continue wrapping. Loops may continue to be added to the "H" to add additional pressure. After completing loops around the "H," continue to wrap the limb, overlapping above, below and on each side of the injury.

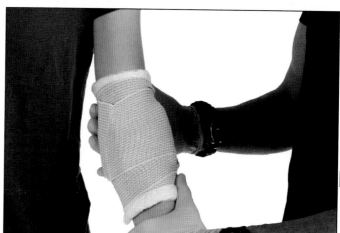

Step 4: Secure the bandage in place with the plastic retaining lock and get the patient to an emergency room as soon as is possible.

Commercial Tourniquets

For severe bleeding from an extremity that cannot be controlled by direct pressure or a pressure bandage, a tourniquet must be applied in order to save the patient's life. Some think applying a tourniquet may seem like it could cause more harm than good. But a 2008 study reviewed tourniquet use in Iraq in 2006, where 232 patients had 428 tourniquets applied on 309 injured limbs. Researchers concluded that tourniquets were medically necessary in 97 percent of the cases, or in all but 12 of the 428 applied tourniquets. That same study addressed the concern that tourniquet use would result in the loss of limbs or that extended use of a tourniquet would damage nerves or cause blood clots, leading to the patient's death. The

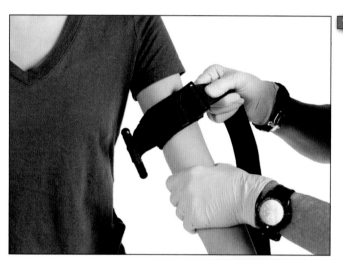

1 Prepare and Position the Tourniquet
Open the strap wide enough to fit the limb through it or disconnect the slip-gate buckle from the strap by twisting it free from the u-shaped clip. Wrap it around the limb and reconnect the slip-gate to the strap.

Place the tourniquet between the injury and the heart (not on a joint) and pull the strap tight.

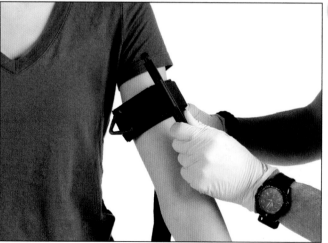

2 Twist Until Bleeding Stops
Twist the aluminum windlass until the bleeding stops. Your patient may complain that the tourniquet is hurting them, but if the artery is continuing to bleed, it isn't tight enough.

study found that the average tourniquet time was 1.3 hours. The researchers concluded that, "No amputations resulted solely from tourniquet use." In one case, a tourniquet remained applied for 14 hours, yet that patient survived. Your patient will have far less time to wait before they are in the hands of EMS professionals, but during that time, applying a tourniquet may just save lives. Modern tourniquets such as the SOF Tactical Tourniquet (Wide) (SOFTT-W), the Combat Application Tourniquet (CAT) and the Ratcheting Medical Tourniquet (RMT) are battlefield-proven and designed to be quickly deployed by either a rescuer or self-applied. The example below demonstrates how to properly apply the SOFTT-W on an upper extremity.

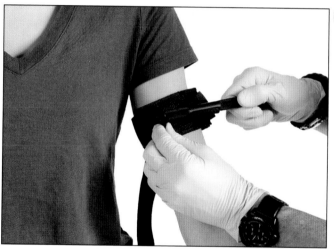

3 Lock the Windlass
Lock the windlass in place using the triangular locking buckle.

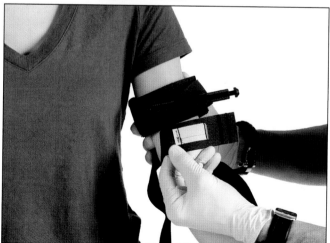

4 Record Time
Note the time that you placed the tourniquet on the white tag, which will be valuable information for the emergency room staff. Under no circumstances should you loosen or remove the tourniquet.

Field-Expedient Tourniquets

While the best solution for stopping uncontrolled arterial bleeding on an extremity is a commercial tourniquet, if you find yourself in a situation where no commercial tourniquet is available, you can fashion a field-expedient one. You need nothing more than a 2- to 4-foot length of cloth, such as a tie, a bandana, gauze, athletic wrap, a scarf, a sock, nylon hose or a wide strip torn from a shirt, and a field-expedient windlass, such as a pen.

Make sure that your field-expedient tourniquet is 1 to 2 inches wide. While TV and movie dramas often show belts used as field-expedient tourniquets, there is typically no easy method of locking a belt in place after it has been tightened, so my suggestion is to use the method explained below instead. In addition, using a cloth that is too thin, such as a shoelace, will only result in severe damage to the patient's skin, muscles and underlying vessels. Even if you have to tear the sleeve off of your shirt, you can find appropriate materials for a field-expedient tourniquet wherever you are.

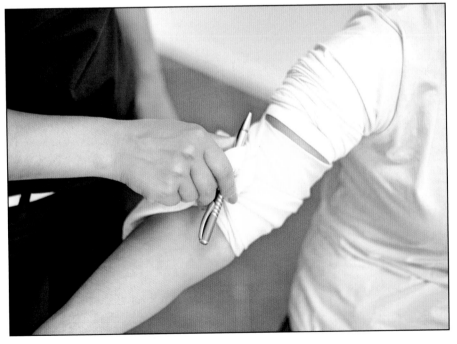

Applying a Field-Expedient Tourniquet

1. Find a cloth that is 1 to 2 inches wide and at least 2 feet long, as well as a thin, solid object that can be used as a windlass, such as a pen.

2. Place the center of the cloth on the back of the affected limb, with an equal amount of cloth extending to the left and the right of the limb.

3. Wrap the limb tightly from both directions. The result should be both tail ends meeting on top of the limb.

4. Tie a single overhand knot on top of the limb. Place your windlass on top of that knot and tie a square knot on top of the windlass.

5. Twist the windlass until the bleeding stops. Tying another cloth over the windlass will lock it in place.

Wound Packing

When a severe gunshot injury is beyond the area that can be treated with a tourniquet, such as in the groin, shoulder or armpit, it may be necessary to pack the injury with sterile gauze (standard or hemostatic) in order to control severe bleeding. Wound packing should only be considered as a last resort and only done if the only alternative is the rapid decline and death of the victim. As a side note, this will be extremely painful if your patient is conscious.

For a deep, penetrating injury in one of these locations, your first step will be to find the lacerated artery and apply direct, significant pressure with a thumb in order to slow or stop the bleeding. Since the wound cavity will very likely be flooded with blood, you may need to soak up blood that has pooled in the wound using rolled gauze and then find the lacerated artery by feel alone. While that might sound difficult, a severely lacerated artery will feel like a high-powered squirt gun and very likely have a "pulse" — as in when the heart beats, blood will gush out. For an extra bit of help for these type of injuries, I recommend that you include a hemostatic gauze "ribbon" in your emergency first-aid supplies.

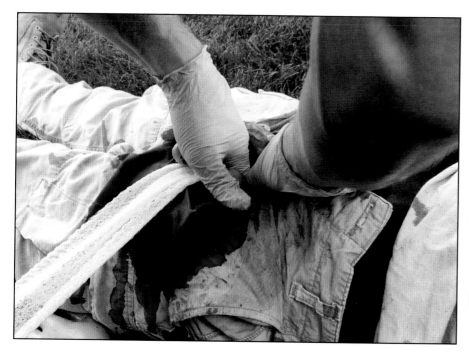

Packing a Wound

1. If you can't visually detect the bleeding artery, feel for it by placing your fingers deep in the wound cavity. Once located, place direct pressure on the bleeder with a thumb or pinch it off with two fingers.

2. Pull gauze out of the center of a roll or from the end of a z-folded gauze ribbon and push it into the wound using a thumb-over-thumb method. Feeding small amounts of gauze into the wound rather than large amounts will result in a more tightly packed wound cavity.

3. Continue to feed gauze into the wound cavity until it is completely filled. As the gauze is fed in, it can be twisted, which will allow it to be even more tightly packed.

4. Once the wound is completely packed, place the remainder of the gauze roll or ribbon over the top of the injury and apply significant pressure to the injury until the patient is handed off to a professional rescuer.

PENETRATING CHEST INJURIES

Penetrating gunshot injuries to the front or back of the torso that have penetrated at least to the pleural space (the layer between the lungs and the chest wall) are referred to as an open pneumothorax. To understand what a pneumothorax is and why it's so dangerous, you have to first understand a bit about the mechanics of breathing.

Ask the average person why the chest rises on inspiration (when a person breathes in), and they'd most likely say that it expands because the lungs fill with air, much the same as how a balloon inflates when air is blown into it. But that's actually incorrect. The opposite is true — the chest doesn't rise because the lungs fill with air, the lungs fill with air because the chest rises.

The chest wall, and the lungs along with it, expand due to the diaphragm and the intercostal muscles (the muscles between the ribs) both contracting. According to Boyle's law, the expanded volume results in decreased pressure inside of the lungs. Air then rushes into the airway to equalize the lower pressure inside the lungs with the higher pressure outside the lungs. On expiration (when the person breathes out), the diaphragm and intercostal muscles relax, and the elastic recoil of the chest increases pressure in the lungs, causing the air to rush out of the airway. In order for the lungs to expand as the chest wall expands, a vacuum must be maintained in the pleural space; there is actually no connecting tissue between the chest wall and the lungs, only a small amount of fluid to reduce friction. When the vacuum in this space is lost as the result of a penetrating injury, the lung will separate from the chest wall during inspiration. Boyle's law once again takes affect as air rushes into the pleural space to equalize the pressure, and a pneumothorax is the result. Even a small amount of air in the pleural space will dramatically increase respiratory effort, which can lead to hypoxia. Larger volumes of air in this space can lead to what's referred to as a tension pneumothorax, or the pleural space completely filling with air. This causes the lung to collapse and increases pressure on the heart dramatically, which can reduce cardiac output and ultimately lead to traumatic cardiac arrest. Classic signs of a tension pneumothorax include a "deviated trachea" — the trachea shifting to the side opposite the injury — a hyper-extended chest and diminished or no lung sounds on the injured side.

Field Treatment

- Upon identifying the sucking chest wound, immediately cover it with a gloved hand. Covering it with the back of your hand leaves your fingers free to prepare a chest seal.
- Check the opposite side of the patient for an exit wound.
- Use a clean towel or sterile gauze to wipe the area clean of blood, sweat or other fluids that might interfere with a tight seal.
- If using a commercial seal, remove the backing and prepare to place the seal. If the seal has a valve, the valve should be placed directly over the penetrating injury. If an exit wound exists, place a second seal over that injury. Apply the seal at the moment of full expiration.

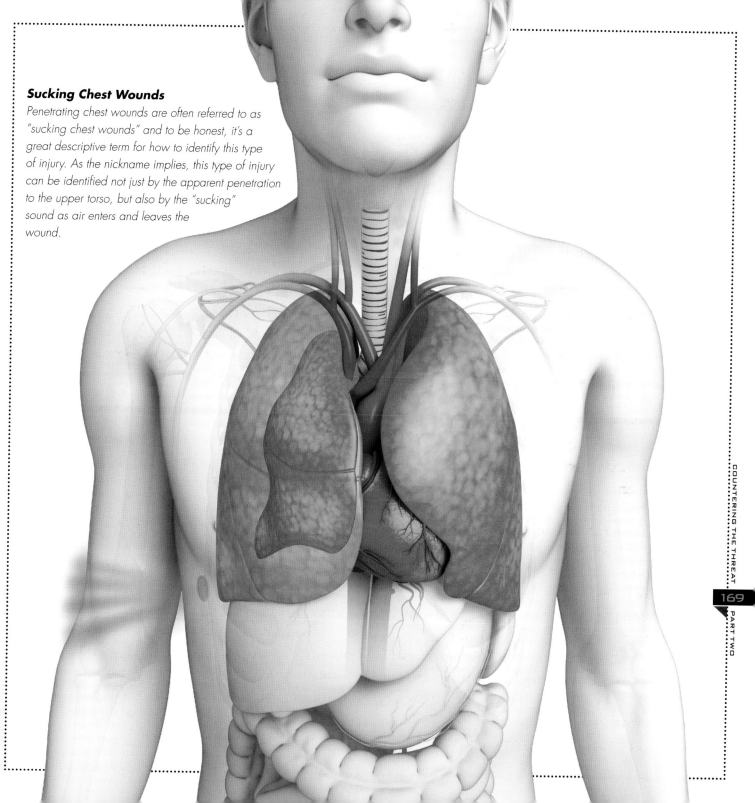

Sucking Chest Wounds

Penetrating chest wounds are often referred to as "sucking chest wounds" and to be honest, it's a great descriptive term for how to identify this type of injury. As the nickname implies, this type of injury can be identified not just by the apparent penetration to the upper torso, but also by the "sucking" sound as air enters and leaves the wound.

- If creating a field-expedient seal, place an occlusive covering, such as a sandwich or other plastic bag, over the injury and tape it on three sides. The open side allows the trapped air to "burp" out while eliminating the introduction of additional air into the pleural space.

- Monitor the patient for signs and symptoms of a tension pneumothorax and "burp" the seal if they appear.

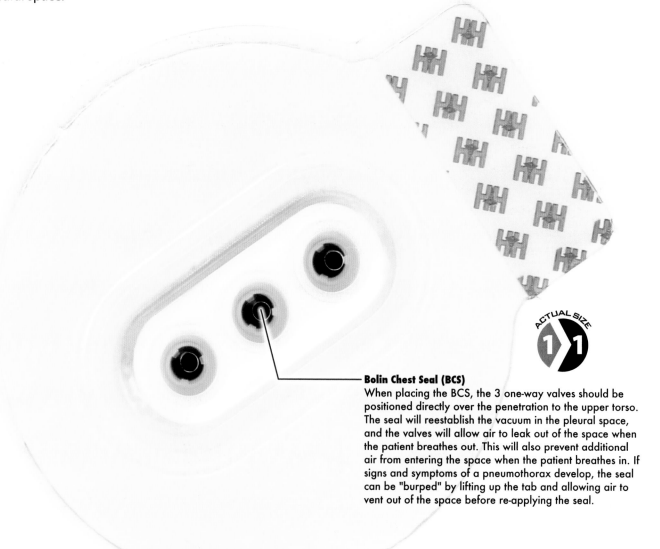

ACTUAL SIZE
1 1

Bolin Chest Seal (BCS)
When placing the BCS, the 3 one-way valves should be positioned directly over the penetration to the upper torso. The seal will reestablish the vacuum in the pleural space, and the valves will allow air to leak out of the space when the patient breathes out. This will also prevent additional air from entering the space when the patient breathes in. If signs and symptoms of a pneumothorax develop, the seal can be "burped" by lifting up the tab and allowing air to vent out of the space before re-applying the seal.

PENETRATING ABDOMINAL INJURIES

Gunshot injuries to the abdominal cavity should be considered very serious life threats, right up there with a penetration to the chest wall. Whenever the abdomen has sustained a gunshot wound, you must assume that an organ or vessel contained within the abdominal cavity has also sustained an injury.

Emergency Care

- Monitor the patient's ABCs and prepare to treat for shock.
- Place the patient in a position of comfort, normally a reclined (or "supine") position. If no injury has been sustained to the lower extremities or the spine, the legs may be flexed at the knees and positioned near the chest, which can reduce the pain experienced by the patient.
- Do *not* allow the patient to eat or drink anything.
- Cover the injury with a sterile dressing or a clean towel that has been soaked with sterile or at least clean water. Place the dressing over any protruding organs and do not attempt to replace the organs back into the abdominal cavity. Cover the moist dressing with an occlusive dressing such as plastic wrap or a plastic bag. This protects the organs from drying out and allows emergency room personnel to save the organs when they might otherwise die.

TREATING FOR SHOCK

Hypoperfusion, a fancy way of saying that the body's cells are not receiving adequate oxygen, glucose and other nutrients because of an interruption in the bloodstream, is commonly referred to as shock. After treating your patient for the specific gunshot injury type and location, you must also aggressively protect your patient from the effects of shock. Unless treated, shock will progress through three stages.

Stages of Shock

Compensatory Shock: As pressure inside the blood vessels drops, the body compensates by releasing hormones in an attempt to increase blood pressure by constricting the blood vessels and increasing heart rate. During this stage, your patient may have a normal blood pressure and an increased heart rate.

Decompensatory Shock: During this stage, the body is no longer able to keep up with the loss of pressure in the vessels, and organs and cells will begin to fail. Your patient may have a rapid heart rate and decreased blood pressure.

Irreversible Shock: Like it sounds, regardless of the interventions, if a patient has reached the stage of irreversible shock, the only result is death.

Maintaining Body Temperature
Since shock can compromise the body's ability to maintain a stable temperature, you should help to maintain body temperature by covering the patient with a blanket.

Signs and Symptoms

- Pale, cool and clammy skin.
- Cyanosis (a bluish tinge to the lips and/or nail beds).
- A delayed capillary refill.
- Weak or missing radial pulses.
- An altered mental status.

Field Treatment

Any field treatment for shock has one underlying goal: to improve the delivery of oxygen and glucose to the brain and other cells. Treatment should be as follows:

- First, treat the underlying condition which is causing the patient to slip into shock.
- Since shock can compromise the body's ability to maintain a stable temperature, you should help to maintain body temperature by covering the patient with a blanket.
- While elevating the patient's legs had been an accepted treatment for many years, that treatment has now fallen out of favor with many EMS agencies.
- Reassure the patient and monitor his or her airway.
- Assess the patient's breathing rate and quality. For patients with no breathing or inadequate rate or volume, begin rescue breaths.

ELIMINATE GUN-FREE ZONES

ALL OF THE SOLUTIONS THAT WE'VE DISCUSSED SO FAR have been solutions that can be implemented at the institutional level. But to make a significant dent in mass shootings, we're going to need to change public policy by eliminating gun-free zones or rethinking the obligation an institution owes to us if it chooses disarmament.

As discussed in Part One, since Columbine, and up to and including the terrorist attacks in San Bernardino and Orlando, 48 mass shootings have occurred with 74 percent of the events and 85 percent of the deaths occurring in gun-free zones where private citizens were either disarmed by state law, school policy, federal law or policy, or by private policy.

The data makes the case that schools, houses of worship, public and private businesses and other locations that advertise themselves as "gun-free" aren't actually keeping themselves safe and are instead doing the exact opposite. It raises an interesting question: Should *anywhere* be gun-free? If so, what responsibility does the governing body of that area or building have for keeping occupants and visitors of the disarmament zone safe?

Before attempting to answer those questions, let's look at a case study of what happens when an institution does not bar concealed carry on its property because of federal or state law, but rather makes the determination to disarm all on its own.

Umpqua Community College

On October 1, 2015, a 26-year-old enrolled at Umpqua Community College fatally shot an assistant professor and eight students and wounded nine others before committing suicide as police closed in. As a self-declared gun-free zone (the state of Oregon allows colleges to decide for themselves whether they'll allow students and/or staff to carry guns, and Umpqua opted to be gun-free), the outcome at Umpqua was really a forgone conclusion. But it didn't have to be since the state of Oregon enjoys one of the highest rates of concealed carry permits per capita, with 6.3 percent of all eligible adults holding permits. With nearly 14,000 students registered at Umpqua and an average student age of 38, there was an opportunity to have more than 800 students and staff members on campus capable of defending themselves and their peers. Instead, for nine long minutes (which coincidentally, is the national average for how long mass shootings last) the only armed individual on campus was the shooter.

Today, most of our nation's colleges all carry that same virtual blinking neon light stating, "no one here will stop you." Allowing eligible students, parents and staff to be armed simply provides them with the same protection on school grounds that they enjoy off campus. Removing school grounds from the "gun-free zone" list will deter the next deranged individual who is angry at the world and looking to take out that rage on innocent and unarmed victims.

The claim that more guns on campus will lead to accidental shootings or shootings of opportunity is without merit. Today, the states of Colorado, Idaho and Utah have laws on the books allowing concealed carry on campus by students who have applied for and received a permit and passed a background check. No incidents have occurred involving these lawfully armed students.

Detractors of this solution have also claimed that allowing students to be armed will create an uncomfortable environment for students who are unarmed. But if you are an Oregonian, ask yourself this: Are you uncomfortable when you relax at Starbucks or browse the aisles at Target? While you might not know it, one out of every 16 adults around you has a concealed carry permit. If a mass shooting were to erupt, what would you hope for? Would you pray that the shooter only had 10-round magazines rather than 30-round magazines? Or would you hope beyond hope that one or more of the 200,000 licensed Oregonians were by your side while you waited the nine long minutes for the police to make entry?

Unpqua Community College obviously chose poorly when it came to the options for allowing or barring concealed carry on campus. But as a public institution, should they have been given the option? For that, let's turn to Kansas as a model.

In an Oregon Court of Appeals case in 2011, a three-judge panel concluded that Oregon public colleges and universities no longer have authority to ban firearms on the physical grounds of a campus. Each school does, however, have discretion as to whether concealed carry will be allowed inside of buildings, dormitories, event centers and classrooms. Unpqua Community College chose to enforce a ban within those areas, effectively making the entire campus a "gun-free zone." The result was that on October 1, 2015, for nine long minutes, the only person on campus with a gun was a mass shooter.

UMPQUA COMMUNITY COLLEGE

WELCOME BACK STAFF AND STUDENTS

FF'S LINE DO NO

177

Since Europe has a longer history of terrorist attacks, European airports have a longer history of extensive armed security. But post-9/11, the U.S. has set the standard for airport security using a two-step standard. Step one, disarm everyone. Step two, protect everyone with armed security.

Photo by Michael Probst / AP

Kansas HB 2052

With the passage of House Bill 2052, Kansas forced the hand of public institutions that wanted to ban concealed carry but with security amounting to nothing more than signs declaring the ban. Today, those public institutions may still choose to restrict the rights of concealed carry permitees from carrying in buildings, but if the institutions do so, "adequate security measures" must be provided to ensure that *no one* (license holders *or* criminals) may carry a firearm or *any* weapon into the building. The theory behind the passage of HB 2052 is best explained by Kansas State Sen. Forrest Knox (R-Altoona):

"Following passage of concealed carry in Kansas, many buildings were posted prohibiting concealed carry even though no security was provided. The recent prevalence of mass shootings in public places, many of which have been posted "no concealed carry" and are often referred to as "gun-free zones," has shown such places to be attractive sites for criminals. Elected officials are realizing that there are liability concerns in posting unsecured buildings.

The 2007 Virginia Tech shooting is an example of such an event. A jury found the school liable in a civil lawsuit and awarded family members of victims large cash settlements. In this case, the judge instructed the jury that a special relationship did exist between university officials and the victims, and that the relationship required officials to provide for their safety and security. The jury found that Virginia Tech's actions contributed to the deaths of the students."

"In America, our right to keep and bear arms is guaranteed, and we must not allow this to be denied anyplace that we have a right to be. The only exception to this is in the rare instances when special security is provided to the general public as a whole. Elected officials and Kansas citizens are figuring out, a sign is not adequate security."
Kansas State Sen. Forrest Knox (R-Altoona)

> *"Kansas [license holders], are not a threat to our security. We should not tread on their rights while at the same time taking no steps to prevent criminals from bringing illegal weapons into public buildings. Good Kansans with guns make all of Kansas safer."*
> **Kansas State Sen. Forrest Knox (R-Altoona)**

"In America, our right to keep and bear arms is guaranteed, and we must not allow this to be denied anyplace that we have a right to be. The only exception to this is in the rare instances when special security is provided to the general public as a whole. Elected officials and Kansas citizens are figuring out, a sign is not adequate security.

Implied in [HB 2052] is that the weapons themselves are not evil but rather it is the actions of criminals that are evil. We can trust the citizens of Kansas and should not limit their freedoms based on the illegal actions of a few. Local control starts with our citizens, by protecting their constitutionally guaranteed individual liberties. Kansas [license holders], are not a threat to our security. We should not tread on their rights while at the same time taking no steps to prevent criminals from bringing illegal weapons into public buildings. Good Kansans with guns make all of Kansas safer."

What HB 2052 Provides

To summarize Senator Knox's outstanding explanation of Kansas HB 2052, publicly owned buildings in Kansas may no longer restrict licensed concealed carry unless "adequate security measures" are present. Adequate security measures mean two things:

1. The use of electronic equipment and personnel at public entrances to detect and prevent the carrying of *any* weapons into the building by members of the general public. Electronic equipment may include metal detectors, metal detector wands or similar equipment used for detecting weapons.

2. Adequate options for storing and securing lawfully carried weapons, such as gun lockers or similar storage devices at all public entrances.

Areas Not Covered by HB 2052

Publicly owned buildings that do not have open access to the public or that have only controlled access entrances are not specifically covered by HB 2052. Examples of this include primary and secondary schools (K-12), which have an automatic exemption to the "adequate security measures" requirement. However, that does not mean that carrying in Kansas primary or secondary schools is automatically banned. It simply means that these schools may choose to post their schools as not allowing concealed carry without meeting the "adequate security measures" requirement. If they choose not to post, then carrying in those buildings is legal for license holders.

In addition, nothing in HB 2052 prevents law enforcement agencies from prohibiting weapons from entering the secure areas of buildings. However, they cannot prohibit licensed concealed carry in the public areas unless they meet the "adequate security measures" requirement.

Government Backed Armed Staff Program

In addition to the changes for posting requirements, HB 2052 also provides certain publicly owned institutions with authority to allow employees who are concealed carry licensees to carry within buildings, even if the buildings are posted.

■ After Kansas HB 2052 became law, publicly owned buildings in Kansas may no longer restrict licensed concealed carry unless "adequate security measures" are present, including the use of electronic equipment and personnel at public entrances to detect and prevent people from bringing of weapons of any kind into the building.

These institutions, which may set their own policy or training requirements for allowing employees to carry, include the following state- or municipal-owned institutions:

- Unified school districts
- Medical care facilities
- Adult care homes
- Community mental health centers
- Indigent health care clinics
- Post-secondary educational institutions

Firearms in K-12 Schools

As mentioned, if a public primary or secondary school in Kansas chooses to post buildings as off-limits for concealed carry, they get an automatic exemption to the "adequate security measures" requirement. But the decision whether or not to ban is left it up to the individual school. The school may choose to allow carry by licensees or it can choose to post signs announcing that carry is not allowed. Or, as mentioned, the school may choose to allow licensed employees to carry, regardless of whether the school itself is posted.

I'll add that after its passage, HB 2052 provided municipalities with a limited exemption for six months in order for security plans to be developed. Thereafter, one four-year exemption was allowed. After this four-year period (which ended on December 31, 2017), no further exemption is allowed. After that date, all state and municipal buildings must either provide the "adequate security measures" as outlined, or they must allow concealed carry licensees to carry.

Using Kansas HB 2052 as a Model

While you might view Kansas HB 2052 as radical, it should really serve as a model for updating the laws in all 50 states. It should serve as an example for all institutions that may decide or have decided to ban lawfully carried firearms on their premises regardless of what state or federal law says, as Umpqua Community College did.

If lawfully armed Americans are going to be disarmed at the front door of any location, we must ask for and expect that our personal security is being ensured by much more than a sign posted at the entrance. Instead, we should expect the same type of "adequate security measures" as defined in Kansas HB 2052.

I would take this a step further. In addition to providing, "electronic equipment and personnel at public entrances to detect and restrict the carrying of any weapons into the state or municipal building," it's also my belief that the responsibility for protecting individuals within any disarmament zone must be borne by the body responsible for disarming them. In other words, if a governing body wants to remove your right to protect yourself with a firearm, it must do two things. First, it must have adequate security to ensure that *no one else* within the gun-free zone may have a gun or *any* weapon. Second, it must provide *armed* security to defend you in the event that an armed intruder is able to make it past security. The sterile area of an airport is a good example. The U.S. government wants these areas to be weapon-free, so it established security at each entrance to that sterile area to ensure that no one carries a gun, knife or any other type of weapon past security. Second, airports provide armed officers throughout the terminal and on many airplanes to provide security for the disarmed masses. Whether you believe that those measures are an adequate defense against a potential mass shooter at an airport or against another terrorist attack on an airplane, it is at least a model for how we should be thinking about disarmament zones elsewhere in the U.S. If your child's school wants to ban you from lawfully carrying a firearm on the premises, then its moral obligation to you and your child is

to ensure that *no* armed person may enter the premises other than the mandatory armed security that the school has put in place. No other option can avoid the nightmare scenario that all mass shooters look for and all parents dread: A building in which everyone has been conveniently disarmed by the authorities, yet still allows an armed attacker to walk right in unopposed.

Due to the recent mass shootings on college campuses, the administration has decided to take swift action to protect our students and faculty by putting up this sign.

YOU SHOULD FEEL MUCH SAFER NOW

In addition, it has also revoked the First Amendment rights for any student wishing to openly advocate for his or her Second Amendment rights. A safe place has been created for any student whose feelings have been hurt by such talk.*

*Not an actual safe place, just a place with cozy chairs and pictures of kittens.

■ While this sign is obviously meant as a parody, it brings to light the foolish belief that signs or school policies will stop mass shootings at colleges or at any other location. Far too many colleges spend more time and money on creating "safe zones" for students whose feelings have been hurt than they spend on actual "safe rooms" or on training the "Run, Hide, Fight" methodology.

WHERE DO WE
GO FROM HERE?

W E'VE COVERED MANY TOPICS IN THIS BOOK.

But reading about these topics is one thing; action is another. I'll challenge you personally to take action by leaving you with six things that you can do to help make a difference.

1. Begin Locally

Attend school informational meetings and ask specifically: What plan does the school have in the event of a mass shooter? Bring the "School Security Checklist" with you and ask how the school expects to address those major gaps in security. Talk about the solution implemented at Southwestern High School in Indiana and ask why a similar system isn't being considered. And finally, encourage other parents to read this book so they can also arm themselves with the facts. The more we can educate the public, the more likely someone will stand up and hit the BS buzzer the next time someone claims that banning AR-15s or 30-round magazines will solve anything.

2. Get Political

Ask your local, state and federal politicians what specific solutions they are proposing to end this scourge. If your representatives are still proposing things like magazine restrictions, banning AR-15s or pushing universal background checks as the panacea, put them on the spot and ask how many lives would have been saved at Sandy Hook or San Bernardino or any of the other 48 mass shootings since Columbine had those solutions had been in place? If they say anything other than none, politely inform them that they're wrong and back it up with the facts from this book. If they're open to education, refer them to this book. It would also be helpful for you to download a copy of Kansas HB 2052 and send it to all of your state representatives. Ask them to sponsor a similar bill in your home state and offer to help organize meetings between them and local gun-rights organizations if that would help the process along.

3. Introduce the "Run, Hide, Fight" Methodology

You need to implement the "RHF" program in your school, house of worship, business and family. After San Bernardino, there's a chance that your company might have introduced the "Run, Hide, Fight" program, but there's almost no chance that your child's school has introduced it, regardless of whether your child is in pre-K, college or anywhere in between. Introduce the program yourself and educate your own family members to the methodology. Ask your child's school administrators if they've heard of the program and ask that it be introduced. Regardless of how far you can get with schools, churches and business, always remember that your safety is your responsibility, and you're the one who needs to prepare in order to be there for your loved ones during a disaster.

4. Question Your Company's Policies

While school shootings certainly have had a major impact on Americans' fear of mass shootings, it's worth noting that since Columbine, 64 people were killed at private businesses with company policies disarming employees, and another 40 people were killed at public businesses that chose to advertise themselves as gun-free zones. Corporate lawyers who are disarming employees and customers over worries about liability should be held liable for the deaths that occur in these locations. Share the ideas in this book about what the value of an armed employee program would bring. Refer to Kansas HB 2052 for how this type of plan is being institutionalized and, as with your representatives, offer to help organize meetings between HR and local gun-rights organizations if that would help the process along..

5. If You See Something, Say Something

Fifth, I'll echo the phrase used by the Department of Homeland Security: If you see something, say something. As discussed in the "Know the Signs" section, in nearly all of the mass shootings that

have occurred in the U.S., the shooters left clues lying around either in what they said, what they were seen doing or what they left floating around in cyberspace. While most perceived threats will turn out to be nothing, you must not take that chance. Alert law enforcement to the facts you have and allow them to investigate. Moreover, if you have a loved one who you believe should be adjudicated mentally ill, it is your responsibility to alert the proper authorities to begin that process. If that is the case, you also need to secure any firearms in a location where that family member has no chance of gaining access.

6. Be a Responsibly Armed American

Finally, my sixth suggestion is for you to become a responsibly armed American. If you don't already have it, get your concealed carry permit, train with your firearm and carry it wherever you're legally allowed. It's worth noting that at the five public locations where mass shootings have occurred since Columbine that were *not* gun-free zones, only one single concealed carry permittee had a gun.

■ *Think that all concealed carry licensees are camouflage-wearing males? Think again. The fastest-growing market segment in the concealed carry world are female permit-holders, with a large percentage falling in the 21-30 age bracket. In conjunction with that growth, the fastest-growing trends in concealed carry products are purses and other carry methods specifically designed for the female market.*

FINAL THOUGHTS

In the original version of this topic published in *Concealed Carry Magazine*, I asked my readers to think about how this argument would change if it were ISIS or Al Qaeda committing these crimes instead of unbalanced domestic terrorists. I suggested that if ISIS or Al Qaeda were to attack a school, the argument of magazine capacity would dry-up overnight. Any politician voting against an armed educator program wouldn't have to wait until the next election to be booted from office. He or she would be thrown from office in mass recall elections supported by both Republicans and Democrats.

While they haven't yet attacked a school, a mass shooting on U.S. soil by foreign-inspired terrorists is no longer theoretical with the ISIS-inspired attacks in San Bernardino in 2015 and at the Pulse nightclub in Orlando in 2016. With those attacks, more and more Americans are beginning to realize how ridiculous it sounds to pretend that things like magazine capacity limitations or universal background checks will have any effect on the plans of these mass murderers, regardless of whether they're foreign or domestic inspired terrorists. While additional solutions may exist, the plans outlined in this book stand a very good chance of ending mass shootings in the U.S. forever. Here's why: Mass shooters want to commit horrible crime and then reach the end of their lives painlessly by their own hands. Of course, that's not just a theory of mine; the FBI agrees. Remember that 42 percent of all mass shooters and 70 percent of school shooters commit suicide in place. Their planning goes something like this:

Step 1) Record and upload a vile video to YouTube or write a rambling manifesto explaining why they hate the world.

Step 2) Enter a gun-free zone and shoot as many innocent men, women and children as they can in five to nine minutes. Continue shooting until they hear sirens.

Step 3) Die painlessly by their own hand.

I believe that if schools, houses of worship and public and private businesses were to implement the steps outlined in this book, potential mass shooters will either give up their plans entirely or skip step two and go directly to step three. As the father of two young sons, I don't care which route they go, I just want them to skip step two. Today, potential mass shooters know that if they walk into a gun-free zone armed with any make, model or caliber of firearm, they will have *complete control* of the situation for enough time to complete their mission and reach the fame that they desire. They have no doubt about this. We need to change their thinking and shake their confidence. We *need* these potential shooters to believe with all their heart that they have no hope of breaking through secured entrances or interior doors, that their mission will end in utter failure, and that their death will be agonizing as they're shot by multiple, armed defenders. Then, and *only* then, will this national nightmare end.